If

Om Swami is a monk who lives in an ashram in the Himalayan foothills. In search of the Truth, he renounced the world and went to the Himalayas, where he realized himself after practising intense meditation.

Om Swami has a bachelor's degree in business and an MBA from Sydney, Australia. His blog, omswami.com, where he writes every week, gets more than a million views annually.

If Truth Be Told

A Monk's Memoir

OM SWAMI

First published in India in 2015 by Harper Element
An imprint of HarperCollins *Publishers*

Worldwide publishing rights: Black Lotus Press

Copyright © Om Swami 2015

P-ISBN: 978-0-9940027-4-7
E-ISBN: 978-0-9940027-1-6

Om Swami asserts the moral right to be identified as the
author of this work.
www.omswami.com

The views and opinions expressed in this book are the
author's own and the facts are as reported by him, and
the publishers are not in any way liable for the same.

All rights reserved. No part of this publication may be
reproduced, stored in a retrieval system, or transmitted,
in any form or by any means, electronic, mechanical,
photocopying, recording or otherwise, without the prior
permission of the publishers.

*With eternal gratitude to my parents,
my brother, Rajan, and my sister, Upasana,
for always standing by me*

Contents

Om bhadraṁ karṇebhiḥ śṛṇuyāma devāḥ,
bhadraṁ paśyemāśabhir-yajatrāḥ.
Sthirair-aṁgais-tuṣṭuvāṁsas-tanūbhiḥ,
vyaśema devahitaṁ yad-āyuḥ.

May we hear only good with our ears and
see only good with our eyes.
O Divine, may we lead a life of contentment and health
and sing thy glories during the life span granted to us.

Rig Veda. 1.89.8

Prologue

We are a rather strange species, if you ask me. Strange because, almost always, we want something different from what we already have. Our capacity to be selfless is as immense as our potential to be selfish. I can vouch for this because I saw myself as a kind person, and didn't think I had it in me to cause pain to my loved ones. Yet, when propelled by my desire, I inflicted it upon them effortlessly.

One morning, I got up, got ready, went to work and did not go back home in the evening. Instead, I boarded a train to take me away from all my certainties, from the people I loved and the wealth I owned. Giving my family no warning, no indication even, I simply walked away although I knew full well it would be a point of no return.

It's not that I didn't think about their feelings. I did, but chose to ignore how they might have felt because I couldn't postpone my inner calling any further. I no longer wanted to get up every morning, work the entire day, come home in the evening, eat my dinner and go to sleep just because everyone else was doing it, because it was considered 'normal'. Who decided what was normal anyway? If I had to live my life by the rules and conditions set by others, what was the goal of *my* life, what was my individual purpose—if there was any?

Before me lay the material wealth I had earned painstakingly over the last decade. But cars, properties and a bank balance were lifeless things at the end of the day. They had always had been. I wasn't born with these possessions and they certainly wouldn't go with me after I died. What was the struggle of life about then? And, whatever it was about, was it worth it?

Countless times, I had given myself the consolation that I would find the purpose of my life one day, but this consolation was wearing thin while my questions beat like muffled drums in my head. With each strike, the sound was getting louder, getting closer. It began to drown out all the music around me: the melodious songs of the birds, the pouring rain, the compassionate words of my mother and the caring ones of my father; nothing was audible anymore, let alone joyous.

Leaving behind everything I had worked towards, razing all that I had built and abandoning everyone I had ever known, I felt indifferent towards my own past. An uninterested stranger. Just as the advancing dawn erases the existence of the night, my departure from the material world wiped away my life as I had known it.

From an Internet cafe, I sent emails to my family and close friends, saying I was going away and didn't know if and when I would return. No emotions, no sentiments tugged at my heart when I deleted my email account, destroyed the SIM card, gave away my phone and broke up with my material life of three decades. Casting away the labels that defined me—son, brother, friend, CEO, MBA, colleague—I walked out of the store and into a new skin.

This new existence was utter nakedness; no, not in physical terms, but in being nothing, having nothing, not even an identity or a name—the life of a monk. It was only in this state of emptiness, as it were, that I could be filled by what I sought most desperately: a true inner life.

ONE

The First Step

I checked out of my lodge and stepped out onto the crowded street. Spotting a cycle rickshaw, I waved it down.

'Where to?' said the rickshaw driver.

'Ghat.'

'Which ghat? There are so many here.'

I wasn't prepared for this. How was I to know there were many ghats in Varanasi?

'Just take me to any ghat.'

'I can't take you to just any ghat, sir. Then you will say this is not where you wanted to go.'

'Alright, name a ghat.'

'Dashashvamedha Ghat.'

'Fine, take me there.'

I hadn't been on a rickshaw since 1995. Back then, fifteen years ago, I was a teenager attracted to, and working towards, materialism. Now, at thirty, I was doing exactly the opposite. The vehicle hadn't changed but the direction had; the person hadn't changed but the priorities had.

I presumed I was headed to a quiet riverside but I couldn't be more wrong. The ghat was crowded beyond description, like an agitated mind crowded with thoughts, like ants gathered on a dead insect.

India was hardly new to me; I had spent the first eighteen years of my life in this country. But, rather naively, I had expected a different India in Varanasi. An old image was locked in my head, an image I hadn't seen but conjured up while reading medieval texts: Kashi by the Ganges, an ancient town full of scholars, saints, tantriks, yogis and other spiritually inclined people.

I roamed about for a while, not knowing where to go. A long time ago, I had heard about Telang Swami, a realized soul who had lived in Kashi more than a century ago. There was supposed to be a monastery at the site of his samadhi. I visualized a quiet monastery by the Ganges, where noble sadhaks sat under the shade of old banyan trees and focused on their sadhana under the guidance of a venerable guru. I enquired, but no one knew anything about the monastery.

I thought of visiting the only other place I'd heard of in this city—Manikarnika Ghat, a cremation ground by the river where dead bodies were burnt round the clock. I hoped to meet some tantrik, sitting there and performing esoteric rituals by the burning pyres. I marched back to the main road and stopped another cycle rickshaw. It was nearly noon and the heat was biting me. I tried to tell myself that it was only mid-March, but this intellectual balm failed to soothe my body.

'Will you take me to Manikarnika Ghat?'

'Yes sir, but I can't go all the way there. I can drop you at the nearest point.'

'How much?'

'Rs 20.'

I hopped into the rickshaw, which moved slowly but steadily on the busy road. Several times, the rickshaw driver had to actually get down to manoeuvre it through the crowd. I noticed he was barefoot even though the sun was spewing fire and the road was like a field of burning coal—it just exuded heat.

'Why aren't you wearing any slippers?'

'They got stolen at the temple the day I bought them.'

'I don't know this area. Please stop by a footwear shop. I'd like to get slippers for you.'

'I'll manage, brother.'

'What is your name?'

'Mahesh Kumar.'

'Don't worry, Mahesh, I'll still give you the money for the ride.'

A little later, I spotted a small shoe shop. Mahesh wasn't keen on stopping, so I practically had to order him to halt. Getting off the rickshaw, I gestured to him to follow me into the shop. He came in after me sheepishly.

'Hello, sir,' the shopkeeper said, and asked me to sit down. I beckoned to Mahesh, who was hovering near the entrance, to join me on the sofa. He did so extremely reluctantly.

A young worker at the shop offered me water.

'Please give it to Mahesh,' I said, 'he's your customer today.'

'Do you want sandals instead of slippers? That may be better,' I said to Mahesh.

'Whatever you think is best.'

The sales assistant went to the back of the shop and returned a few minutes later with a pair of sandals. Beige in colour, with dark-brown straps and shining steel buckles, they looked very comfortable. He handed Mahesh the pair.

'Please put them on his feet like you would do for any other customer,' I said.

Mahesh looked at me nervously. I looked into his eyes and nodded. Immediately, his face broke into a smile and he stuck out his feet so that the assistant could put on the sandals. I looked at Mahesh's beautiful, dark face, his yellow teeth, slightly deformed and stained, his big eyes full of contentment, and felt very warm inside. His smile simply made my day.

Mahesh pedalled with renewed enthusiasm now, while his dusty, worn feet seemed to come alive in the new sandals. As I watched his feet pushing the pedals up and down, everything else faded for a moment—the shops, the noise, the heat. All I could see were those feet, which seemed to be performing a cosmic dance. Now a pedal went up and now a pedal came down; every movement seemed effortless, in perfect synchronization.

Mahesh dropped me off at the point closest to Manikarnika Ghat.

'If you go to the temple again, don't leave your shoes outside,' I warned as I got off the rickshaw.

'I won't,' he said.

I offered him a fifty-rupee note.

'How can I take money from you, sir?'

'Please keep this. It will give me great joy if you do.'

He came around from his rickshaw and reached down to touch my feet. I caught his wrists and pulled him up. 'There are only three places you should bow your head,' I said. 'In front of God, in front of the elderly and in front of your guru.'

I thrust the money into his hands and walked away, thinking that Mahesh was not designed to be a rickshaw driver. He could have been a clerk, a watchman, an officer, an executive. For that matter, no one deserved to live a life that sought to break the body as well as the spirit. This man was living in a democratic country but did that make him a free man? The state did not provide for him and his fellow countrymen did not respect him. He did not have the freedom to own a roof over his head or break away from the harshness and drudgery of his daily routine. I don't think Mahesh ever took a vacation or enjoyed any luxury in his life except perhaps the luxury of needs; he would never run out of needs. Come to think of it, there was no difference between him and me: we were both fettered by our needs. His were more tangible and essential for survival, while mine were more abstract and self-imposed.

I navigated my way to Manikarnika Ghat. I doubt if anywhere else in India there existed such tight streets as in Varanasi; at least, I'd never seen them. If you had a slightly bigger nose and turned your head, you were likely to hit something. Well, almost. I don't know how I managed to reach Manikarnika Ghat, but I finally did.

A pyre was burning; another had been mostly reduced to ash, occasionally lit up by smouldering embers. Pieces of broken clay pots lay scattered around. Breaking a pot full of water at the time of cremation is a Hindu custom signifying that the soul of the deceased has severed all ties with the human world. The pot symbolizes the human body, and its breaking indicates the liberation of the soul that has trapped within.

There were no saints to be found here, no practitioners of the occult sciences, no evolved tantriks or yogis who beckoned to me to join them in a journey to self-realization. Instead, around the pyres, dealers sat selling wood; beside them sat paanwallahs and chaiwallahs. Milling around were countless people, cows, dogs and cats.

The ghat had turned out to be a disappointment, so I began asking about Telang Swami's monastery again. Of the many souls I asked, one seemed to know. He pointed in a certain direction. I walked down narrow streets with decrepit buildings ready to crumble and shops selling all manner of things. Dodging the maddening traffic, I found myself in winding alleyways, going past houses standing cheek-by-jowl and children playing beside parked two-wheelers, doing my best to avoid stepping into puddles of animal urine and dung.

After forty-five minutes, feeling tired and hopeless, I stopped. I couldn't see the monastery and I couldn't find anyone who had ever seen it. I sat down on the kerb and wiped the sweat off my forehead, wondering how to proceed. After a few minutes, I raised my head and there it was, on my right, a sign written in Hindi: 'Telang Swami Math'. It was a temple.

I went inside. A middle-aged man was sitting on the pujari's seat. Everything about him was round—head, face, torso, belly, hands, feet. A barber came in behind me, took his kit out of his bag and began shaving the priest. I watched quietly, enjoying the coolness of the temple after the searing heat outside. After a few minutes, the barber picked up his things and left; no money exchanged hands. Perhaps they had some kind of monthly arrangement.

I asked the priest about Telang Swami and his lineage, and about the monastery. He said there was no disciplic succession or ashram. This temple was all there was and there was no arrangement for anyone to stay even if they could pay.

I felt betrayed, although I was not sure by whom.

'Telang Swami is buried there.' He pointed to a corner of the temple compound. Walking across to Telang Swami's tombstone, I prayed, 'Please guide this lost soul, O Swami, so I may attain what I've set out to do.'

On my way out, the priest stopped me to ask exactly what I was looking for. I told him I was in search of a guru and wanted to take sanyasa diksha, initiation into the life of a renunciant. He said there was no need to renounce the world or look for a guru, and that I should get married and lead a normal life.

Normal life? There's nothing called a normal life. What is normal from one's viewpoint may be most abnormal from another's. A yogi thinks that the world is abnormal and people live like animals, mostly focused on feeding and fornicating. The world thinks the yogi is a fool who wastes his life sitting around doing nothing, enjoying none of the many pleasures life has to offer.

Naturally I didn't say any of this to the priest. I had no interest in pursuing a conversation with someone who could understand neither my desperation nor my intention.

I went towards the ghats again. It was nearly 3 p.m. and the sun was even hotter now. I hadn't eaten anything all day. In the morning, I hadn't been able to find any place to eat where the food wasn't deep-fried. In the afternoon, I was busy with my self-realization business. My water bottle had been empty for hours and the reality of hunger was tugging hard at my stomach.

Lacking a sense of direction, I didn't know if I was heading towards the ghats or away from them. When I saw the number of people on the streets reduce significantly, I knew I was heading in the wrong direction. Coincidentally, I saw some lodges there and asked a few if they had any vacancy. I just wanted to lie down in a cool, quiet place. Oddly enough, at each place, they asked me where I was from, how many people needed the room and for how many days. Then they would tell me there was no room available. I was intrigued. Why would they put me through a whole heap of questions if they had no room available?

I walked on and eventually found myself by the river. The Hindu texts talked a great deal about the sacred significance of 'Ganga Maiya'. Well, her 'children' had polluted her beyond imagination. Seeing the filthy state of the river flowing past me, I shook my head in as much disgust as disbelief. I had seen the Ganga till Haridwar, where it was clean, but what had happened here in this holiest of holy cities, the Kashi of my imagination? I decided I would not bathe in the river here. Inwardly though, I paid obeisance to the sacred Ganga. A ma remains a ma, no matter how she's dressed.

'Massage?' I looked up to see a man standing near me.

'No massage. I need a guide.'

'Sure, sir. I'll be your guide.'

'You do know this area well?'

'Yes, sir.'

'What will you charge? I need you with me for the rest of the day. And maybe tomorrow as well.'

'You can pay whatever you like.'

'Rs 250 per day?'

'Okay, sir.'

'Let's go.'

'I'll take your bag,' he offered kindly.

It took me a few minutes to realize I was free of the load. That's the thing with baggage—you get used to carrying it around. You know it's heavy but the weight has a way of becoming a part of your life. Only when you take it off your back and feel the lightness does the awareness of the load hit you.

Manish took me to a couple of guest houses and I got the same questions there too. Finally, my guide solved the mystery for me by explaining that when the employees at these lodges weren't busy with work or occupied watching a cricket match on TV, they longed to chat with people as a way of passing their time. They didn't have any rooms available but a conversation with a stranger was welcome.

Not getting very far in my search for a place to stay, I asked Manish to take me to a bigger hotel, but he said there wasn't one. I realized that he didn't really know the area; he had lied to me. Anyway, I was starving now. We managed to spot a vegetarian Jain dhaba that served meals without onion or garlic. I avoided eating onion and garlic, so the menu was fine with me but the food wasn't; it was tasteless. I was too tired to fuss and my head hurt. I swallowed whatever I was served, though my guide seemed to savour the meal. After we left the dhaba, I bought two chilled bottles of water from a small provision store. Opening the first one, I washed my face and poured the rest on my head. The second I guzzled right away.

It was nearly 6 p.m. by the time we resumed our hunt for accommodation, and we finally got lucky at Pooja Guest House, where they gave me a room. I let Manish go and asked him to come again the next morning.

Even though I had a room now, I couldn't sleep because of the fatigue and dehydration, which was evident from the colour of my urine. I hadn't known I was so fragile. There was a time not long ago when I had played badminton daily, spent hours at a stretch on the golf course, pumped iron and run 12 miles regularly, and all this had felt effortless. But today, just one day spent in the 'real' world, and I found myself stretched beyond what I could take. My belief that I was fit and strong seemed merely a conceited notion.

I realized that my body was far from ready for the hardships of monkhood. If I couldn't even tolerate the heat of a day, what chance did I have to endure the rigours of meditation and the harsh life of an ascetic? I had no idea how to prepare my body for intense penance. Yet, I knew that life would teach me. I had only to be open and willing.

I lay there thinking about my worldly journey thus far.

TWO

The Mystic

M y mother was raised in a deeply religious environment
and grew up revering religious figures. She would
never lose an opportunity to seek the darshan of mystics
and saints who visited our town.

One day, during the lunch hour at work, she went to get
the blessings of an unusual saint she had been told about.
It was said that he never slept; he didn't even blink. He
observed silence most of the time. Perpetually wandering,
he wouldn't stay more than one night in a place, and never
returned to the same town again.

'In the month of Margashirsha, when the moon is waxing,
you will give birth to a special soul,' he said as soon as he
saw my mother.

My mother was brought up not to question saints, but
she wasn't expecting this blessing from the mystic who
rarely spoke.

'Babaji, I already have two children.'

'It doesn't matter,' the sadhu said. 'One of us is coming
after a long wait. A saint.'

My mother's heart sank. One of them? A saint?
That meant he wouldn't lead a normal life but give up

everything. She lowered her head and sat quietly, trying to calm herself.

'Yes, he will renounce,' he said, reading her mind. 'Please remember me when he is born, and touch some tulsi leaves to his lips as an offering from me.'

She bowed before him and got up to leave. Her thoughts were in turmoil. Her family was already complete and there was no need to have a third child. Yet, the thought of losing this third child, to have him become a wandering sadhu, was unbearable.

'You are merely the medium. Don't resist the ways of the Divine,' the saint said as he gave her a pinch of holy ash. 'Eat this ash on ekadashi. At his birth, petals will shower from above and a rainbow will be seen.'

My birth might have been foretold but it certainly wasn't planned, my father would tell me later. After losing their first child, my parents had gone on to have a boy and a girl, and were neither planning nor hoping for a third child. But, fifteen months after the holy man's prediction, in the month of Margshirsha, on the twelfth night of the waxing moon, I was born in a government hospital.

Except for a light drizzle, nothing else fell from the sky and there was no rainbow in sight. I was delivered before my father or other relatives could even reach the hospital. The customary gutti, the giving of honey to the newborn baby, usually done by mother's brother, was given by a nurse instead. My mother had remembered to carry the tulsi with her though. Squeezing three leaves between her thumb and fingers, she touched the juice to my lips. My father reached half an hour after I was born and named me Amit.

Hoping she might avoid what was written in the book of fate, my mother kept the mystic's prediction to herself. It was only after my renunciation more than thirty years later, when she saw me in my ochre robes, that she would reveal what had transpired long years ago.

≈≈≈

The years went by, and I was now five. The summer vacation had just started. One day, my parents were at the office while my siblings and I were at home. Rajan and Didi were playing outside but I wasn't interested in their games. Looking for something else to occupy me, I began browsing through the cupboard in the living room and came upon a stack of comics in the bottom shelf. Curious, I sat down on the floor and began to flip through the pages.

Within moments, I was entranced by the attractive illustrations though I didn't think I could read the sentences. But, when I paid attention to the dialogue bubbles, much to my surprise, letter by letter, word by word, the sentences formed. This was my first experience of reading sentences.

My mother used to tell me bedtime stories every night, but I now discovered a whole new world of stories. Every word I read filled me with an inexplicable joy and I remember giggling as I read. It was as if a narrator was talking to me personally, telling me those wonderful tales. I felt I was walking with someone through a dark forest, being guided by the lamp he was holding up for me. With every step we took, the space before us lit up and a whole new world unfurled. I sat there reading one issue after another as the morning rolled by.

Finally, Didi came in to ask me to eat; it was lunchtime. I ignored her. I didn't want food, I wanted stories. She came again and then again, and I sent her away each time. She was only eleven herself but, being the eldest, was responsible for giving me the lunch my mother had made for us before leaving for work.

'It's already 4 p.m. You must have your lunch now.'

I kept reading.

'Amit?'

I didn't answer.

'Amit! I'm talking to you.'

'I don't want to eat.'

She gave me a peck on my cheek and said, 'It's very late. Please, have your lunch.'

She knew it was impossible to push me into anything even if it was in my own interests. Love was the only way.

'Okay, after five minutes.'

'You've been saying that all day.'

'I promise this time.'

Didi came back half an hour later and the same conversation took place: I asked for more time. But she was having no more of this behaviour. Heating my lunch, she brought it to me.

'I'm not hungry,' I said without looking at her.

'Please, you must eat,' she said. 'Mummy and Papa will be home soon.'

'I must finish my comics, Didi. Please don't disturb me.'

She prepared a bite of chapatti, vegetables, lentils and pickle and brought it close to my mouth, just below my nose. My mouth watered, and I let her put the food into my mouth, reading all the while. I don't know how many chapattis she fed me but I ate whatever she gave. I kissed her cheek and went back to reading. It was my favorite habit, kissing my mother and sister every morning and evening. On the days I was happier, I did so more frequently. They looked after me with great love and I always felt secure and happy with them.

As she got up to take my plate away, Didi said, 'I'm glad you ate. Mummy will be relieved.' My parents worked in the same government organization, though in different departments. For nearly three decades, they had left the house together every morning and returned together in the evening. My father drove a scooter while my mother sat sideways behind him in a ladylike fashion. Patiala was a small town and their office was only fifteen minutes away. Like my parents, half of this town worked for the state electricity board; the other half worked for a nationalized bank. Or something like that.

One day, our family of five went out for dinner. Next to the restaurant was a shop outside which scores of magazines and comics were on display. Within, shelf upon shelf was crammed with books from floor to ceiling. I didn't know such places existed, and was overwhelmed at the sight of these books. I was a tiny piece of iron and here was a giant magnet: it was impossible to resist and I couldn't think of anything else. My dinner, the restaurant, my family—all of it ceased to matter. I had to be in that bookshop and have every comic and magazine of my interest. My father promised to take me there after the dinner but I couldn't wait. I insisted on going right away, and he finally gave in.

Till now, I had only seen magazines and comics being delivered at home with the newspaper. I hadn't even realized you had to buy them separately; I thought they just came with the newspapers. Buy. This was the keyword. You needed money to buy them. If I had a lot of 'rupees', I could have bought all the books in the shop.

Back at the restaurant, I couldn't stop adoring the magazines I just bought. At home, I couldn't sleep because I wanted to read them. At school the next day, I couldn't concentrate because I wanted to get back home and read.

The more comics and magazines I read, the more I wanted to read. My obsession only got worse with time. Whenever my parents wanted to buy something for me, I asked for books.

But how many could they buy after all? There was a limit. So, my first visit to the library was scheduled. It was nearly 5 km away from our home and, on my way there, I felt like an astronaut on his first space trip. When I entered the library, the visual stimulation and intellectual arousal I experienced at the sight of so many books was beyond what my little mind could assimilate. I looked at the librarian and thought he was the luckiest man in the world, for he could read all these books. He had no smile on his face though.

Almost daily, I read for a couple of hours at the library, took two books home, finished them and exchanged them the next day for two more. Two was the limit per person.

'Do you actually finish the books you take home every day?' The librarian asked me once.

'Yes, I do.'

'What's the rush? Why don't you enjoy them and read them slowly?'

'I do enjoy them, Uncle. But I want to read all the books in this section.'

He laughed. 'No one has ever done that.'

He was right. I never got around to reading every book in the children's section. Still, after all the time I spent there, and twelve library cards, more than fourteen hundred books and two years later, he gave me a box of sweetmeats.

***

Many tales in the various magazines and books I read featured gods who would slay demons, create miracles, grant boons and help those who prayed to him. He could fly, he could appear and disappear at will, he could shift shapes ... he could do anything he wished. And every story I read, I assumed to be true. I started building my world around God, with God, in God. I wanted to see him, I wanted to talk to him. I didn't like him being invisible. Perhaps God had appeared before people in ancient times, and maybe it was no longer possible to see him. An incident, however, changed my perception.

One evening when I came back into the house after playing outside, I saw my mother sitting by the altar reading a thick book. I threw my arms around her and kissed her.

'What are you reading, Mummy?'

'*Ramcharitmanas*. The story of Lord Rama.'

'Haven't you finished it yet? You are always reading this book.'

She laughed. 'This is our holy book, son, this is about God. Each time I read it, I receive something new.'

'Is Lord Rama God?'

'Yes.'

'Then what about Lord Shiva and Lord Krishna?' I pointed to the two pictures at the altar.

'They are all God, the same God, just different names, different forms.'

'Where is he then? Why can't I see him in real life?'

'He is everywhere. Those pure of heart see him, those who worship him see him.'

'But you worship him. Why don't you see him?'

'My worship is not the purest. Sometimes, I have to tell a lie and God doesn't like lying. Only those who always speak the truth see him.'

'Why do you have to lie sometimes, Mummy? And can I see him too?'

'Yes, why not?' And she narrated the story of the five-

year-old prince, Dhurva, who went to the woods to pray to
Lord Vishnu and saw a manifestation of the Divine form.
I shivered.

'Can I read this book as well?'

'Of course, I'll read it with you.'

'No. Don't read it with me. Only help me if I get stuck.'

That day, she was reading the Uttar Kand, the last chapter
of the *Ramcharitmanas*, and I glanced at the page she was
on. She told me that it was the 'Rudrashtakam', a eulogy
to Lord Shiva. It was written in simple Sanskrit. Since
Hindi and Sanskrit shared the same script, I began reading.
After some sentences, I got stuck at a long word: 'saffurna-
mauli-kalolini-charuganga'. My mother helped me with the
pronunciation and told me that it meant 'from the matted
locks on Shiva's head gushes forth the beautiful Ganga'.

I didn't know what the eulogy meant but the rhythm
and the sound drew me in. I felt different, as if something
had melted within me. From devouring candies to being
awake well past my bedtime, I had experienced various
kinds of childish delights and felt good on many occasions,
but this was a different feeling altogether. This was not a
wave of happiness that rose and ebbed but the gentle flow
of a river, a river of strange joy. It seemed to me that I had
just experienced God. For the first time, I sensed that it was
possible to see him.

I used to sleep with my mother and demanded a story
every night. She knew countless legends from various
scriptures. That night, she narrated the story of Krishna
and his childhood friend, Sudama. Krishna loved him
deeply and granted the poverty-stricken Sudama material
comforts in the blink of an eye. Moved by the beautiful
story, I slept with thoughts of God and with the conviction
that he did exist.

A fair-complexioned Shiva with a slightly bluish throat appeared in my dream that night. His face was exquisite, his nose sharp and his lips pink and full; silver earrings hung from long ears. Matted locks were tied in a knot on top of his head and his broad shoulders glistened with drops of water, as if he had just come from the snowy Himalayas and the snowflakes had melted on his skin. In one of those drops of water, I saw my own reflection. He gazed at me with soft, loving eyes.

'I've come to see you,' he said.

'Oh, you are Lord Shiva. You must meet my mother.'

He smiled and stroked my head tenderly, his fingers long and slender.

'I've only come for you.'

'No, you must meet my mother, please. She really wants to see you. She prays to you every day.'

But he, the foremost yogi, disappeared.

I woke up my mother.

'Lord Shiva came, Lord Shiva came! I asked him to wait for you but he didn't.'

Then I began crying. 'I asked him to wait. I wanted you to see him. He was so beautiful. God was here, Mummy, Lord Shiva was here.'

She sought to pacify me but the more she tried, the louder I cried. I couldn't bear for her to be excluded from my dream, not belong to a place where God and I existed but she didn't. I could not imagine a life without my mother.

'Stop crying, son,' she said lovingly. 'I'll pray to Lord Shiva to wait for me the next time.'

'Was it real? Did he really come? Are dreams real, Mummy?'

'Yes, of course it was real.'

Even though I was barely eight summers old at the time, I still remember how I had felt that night. I couldn't go back to sleep, not because my mind had any questions but because I was already in a state of deep tranquility — beyond sleep. Such was the touch of Shiva. I started to lose the sense of my individual self and felt I was becoming one with the vast and silent ocean that looked up at the endless sky. There were no boundaries and no resistance, only the expanse of blue ocean and sky, only peace, light and joy. My young body of a few years had just discovered my million-year-old soul.

⁂

A couple of years went by. Ten now, I had stopped reading comics and moved on to books. On the outside, I was mostly happy but, deep within, I craved to see God again, not in a dream but in full consciousness. I found myself deeply restless. I didn't just want to know more about him; I wanted to *know* him because I believed only he could answer the questions that dogged me constantly: Why was the world the way it was, and why was I the way I was? Why was it that some people lived in big houses while others slept on the road? Why did people fall ill and die?

Neither my friends nor my elders could hold a reasoned conversation with me, much less address these questions. Nearly a year passed as I searched in vain for answers. I finally turned to numerology, astrology and other esoteric disciplines, hoping they would bring me the clarity I sought. My mother knew a learned Brahmin, Pandit Suresh Sharma, who agreed to teach me astrology. From him, I understood the significance of the planets and planetary positions. He taught me how to draw the charts, how to normalize zodiac signs based on longitude and latitude and so on.

I studied all the major classical and contemporary works on astrology. These books had explanations and even remarkable insights for me, but no answers. I had read that the sages—authors of the classical astrological texts—had received divine knowledge by way of divination. Clearly, they must have had a way to receive and interpret that knowledge. Why did the Divine talk to them and not to me? The seers who wrote marvellous works of great profundity and foresight had something in common: living in secluded spots in mountains and forests, they chanted Vedic hymns and meditated on God. I couldn't go and live in the woods but I could sit still and try to meditate on God, I thought. I began meditating at every available opportunity even though I had no real guidance or practical understanding of meditation. My method at the time was to sit still and chant 'Om'. That's what I did. Whenever I had an hour to spare, I meditated.

A subtle change did start to come about. I often found myself at the intersection of time where the lines between the past, present and future blurred. It was like déjà vu but with one difference: I could see what the next moment would hold. Just as a flash of lightning illuminates the dark sky for a moment and you see everything around you in its full glory, these flashes of intuition revealed to me information about the person sitting before me that I simply didn't know.

Sometimes, visitors would come for readings and I would know their questions even before they had started speaking. At times, I would be walking in the street and would get similar guidance about a complete stranger walking on the road. I wasn't just seeing people but seeing through them.

I wasn't sure how to label this phenomenon. I called it intuition but there was a small problem with my intuition: it was wild and free. It ran its own course and I had no control over it. Even though it worked, I couldn't call upon it with conviction or at will, nor replicate it whenever I wished. I wanted a more logical sequence, a degree of certainty. I needed my inner guide to answer my questions and not just give me random information about a stranger on the road, no matter how accurate that was.

In the meantime, word spread about my readings in astrology and more and more people started approaching me. Going to school, reading, meditating and meeting people made my schedule rather hectic and there was little time left to play. I didn't mind this because, being asthmatic, I could not engage much in physical sports. There were no inhalers back then, not until I turned fourteen anyway.

For four months every year, March–April and September–October, I was particularly sick. There was a high level of allergens during these months and the medication would take a while to ease my breathing. For long hours at night, I used to sit outside with my mother because lying down made breathing even more difficult. Resting in her lap under a moonlit sky, sometimes a dark sky, I used to look up and wonder about the vastness before me, the countless stars it held, some twinkling more than the others. The questions would come flooding back: Who made the universe? Why was I here and not on one of the other planets? Did people live on other planets too? Did God live on one of those distant stars? Where *was* God?

Minute by minute the hours would pass and my wheezing would finally subside by the morning. Only then would I manage to fall asleep. My father would pick me up and carry me back to my bed. Often, inhaling the air outside wouldn't work and he would rush with me to the hospital. I didn't mind going because spending a night at the hospital meant getting a day off from school. I would stay back at home and catch up on my reading or meditate. An injection in the hospital was a small price to pay for these delights.

≈≈

I had learnt the basic Vedic chants from my astrology teacher, but he only specialized in astrology and didn't have the phonetic precision required in Vedic chanting. I felt it was essential to chant the Vedic hymns in the correct manner in order to continue my exploration and experimentation. It was not enough to just sit still and chant Om. I turned to my mother again, who knew a young but scholarly Brahmin called Pandit Surya Prakash Sharma. He had recently moved to our town.

Over the next few weeks, Panditji taught me the correct and rhythmic pronunciation of the core hymns from the Yajur Veda, one of the four Vedas. Verses from the Yajur Veda are used in the invocation of various forms of divine energies. Sanskrit, the language in which the Vedas are written, has the ability to take the mind into a trance-like state. This is chiefly because of the use of rhyme, rhythm and nasal sound across various meters. So, Panditji agreed to teach me Vedic chanting. My work with him, however, didn't last very long.

Occasionally, people visited him for horoscope readings. Astrology was not his forte although his scholarly excellence in Vedic literature would have anyone believe that he was an expert in astrology too, for astrology was a Vedanga, Vedic branch, after all. One day, a man came to have his daughter's horoscope matched. He had identified a suitable groom for her and wanted to ensure that the horoscopes of the two were compatible. Panditji calculated incorrectly and concluded that it was a flawless match.

The maximum possible 'points' you can score during the matching of horoscopes is thirty-six. Panditji's total came to forty-three. He told the man that forty-three meant it was far better than the accepted thirty-six. I was alarmed. Though just twelve years old at this time, I corrected my teacher and informed him that this match yielded only twelve points, with two doshas, faults. It was actually a terrible match. The man was furious with me and shut me up, saying that Panditji was absolutely right and that such an excellent match was indeed possible because his own horoscope tallied at thirty-three points with his wife's.

He was happy to believe Panditji's incorrect interpretation since it gave him comfort and the permission to go ahead with solemnizing the alliance, something he so wished. This is what happens with most people: they are not in search of truth, they don't want to know the truth; in fact, they are scared of the truth. They have an idea or belief that brings them solace and they merely want someone to validate it for them. They will run hither and thither until someone agrees with them.

'I can't teach you,' Panditji said after the man left.

'Oh, what happened?' I didn't realize he was upset with me.

'Who are you to correct me? You think you are some great astrologer?'

'I'm sorry, please forgive me. But if this man goes ahead and ties the nuptial knot based on the matching today, this marriage will be doomed. I was only trying to help.'

'I know. But you should not have corrected me in his presence. It was insulting and inappropriate.'

'I'm sorry, Panditji.'

'Don't argue with me. I won't teach you anymore. Go
elsewhere.' He added sarcastically, 'You are a Brahmin, a
learned astrologer. You don't need a teacher.'

I touched his feet and walked out of his life. We had both
hurt each other: I had hurt his ego and he had hurt my dream.
I decided I didn't need hymns and astrology; I would go my
own way. Over the next few months, I studied major texts
on yoga, tantra and mantras for guidance, and concentrated
on my meditation. My sadhana yielded some results in the
form of an even sharper intuition, better memory and some
visions and hallucinations, but these gains were nowhere
near what esoteric literature promised.

Treatises on mantra science made remarkable, even
unreal, claims. From flying in the air to the physical
manifestation of objects, these books said all was possible.
It's not that I was particularly interested in these powers but
they were like milestones on the path. When you passed
them, you knew you were headed in the right direction.
This time around, I couldn't find anyone to help me—no
saint, teacher, priest or astrologer. I even started to think
there was little or no truth to these texts on mantra science.
Until, one day, when a dream woke me up to another
reality. A sadhu, tall, bearded and robed in black, appeared
in the dream.

'Keep going, son,' he said.

'Is there any truth to mantras?'

'Spiritual practice and doubt are like light and darkness.
They don't go together. Have faith.'

'I'm not getting any results.'

'Continue with patience and discipline.'

'I've got no one to guide me.'

'I'll visit you before midday today.'

'Please, I want to ask you some questions now.'

But the sadhu disappeared. I woke up, calm and restless all at once. I could not ignore this dream; it was so real and vivid. I ran to my mother who was already up and about although it was still dark outside. She had lit the morning lamp at the altar and was offering prayers to the deities.

'I don't think I should go to the school today,' I interrupted her.

'You're up early. Oh, you've come here without taking a bath?'

Ignoring what she said, I sat down next to her.

'I had a dream, and I think I should stay at home today.'

'Why? Don't be scared.'

'I'm not scared. I saw a sadhu baba in a dream. He said he would visit me today.'

'You must go to school, Amit. Besides, dreams are not real.'

'What are you saying? When I had the dream of Lord Shiva, you said it was real. You said dreams were real. I'm sitting at the altar, Mummy, you know I won't lie to you. It *was* a real dream. I must stay at home because he said he would come today. I promise I'll study during the day.'

'What will I tell your father?'

'Please, please. Tell him anything. He'll believe you.'

'See, you asked me the other day why I lie. This is why I have to lie sometimes!'

We negotiated with each other. Finally, she allowed me to take the day off. Somehow, she managed to convince my father.

Later that morning, I was alone at home. At around 10 a.m., someone knocked at the door. I rushed open it. Standing before me was a sadhu in black robes, matted locks tied at the back of his head and a beard that reached his chest. I offered him alms but he said he had only come to see me. He didn't mention anything about my dream though.

He put his hand into his jhola and pulled out something. Handing it to me, he told me it was a siyar singhi.

A siyar singhi is a little lump that grows on a jackal's body. After it becomes the size of a betel nut, it sheds on its own. There are many tantric applications of a singhi, provided a good tantrik knows how to consecrate it well. It is used to fulfil material goals, cure diseases and hypnotize or mesmerize people. It can also be used in black magic to inflict harm or injury. If you put a genuine singhi in vermilion powder, the hair on it continues to grow steadily and you have to add to the vermilion powder every few weeks to keep it effective. Even though it is a dead lump, it consumes the powder.

'This object is amogha, foolproof. I've come to give it to you,' he said, and briefly explained how I was to use it.

I asked, 'Why am I not getting any siddhi?'

'Because you are not focusing on the ultimate goal but hankering after petty attainments. If you get hold of the sun, you'll get light automatically.'

He reiterated the instructions for the use of the singhi and prepared to leave. I wanted to ask him so many questions but his overwhelming and charismatic presence left me speechless. All I could do was prostrate in reverence. He blessed me and went his way.

There was a lady who used to come to our house daily to do the household chores. She was more like a family member and we called her 'Masi'. My mother did treat her like a loved one. That was an incredible quality about my mother: she was always giving. I never saw her express any hatred, jealousy or anger. She never shouted at us or even raised her voice.

Masi had two sons; the elder one was seven years old and had been suffering from leprosy since birth. I decided to use the singhi on the child. Over the next week, I prepared the singhi for application by consecrating it with a mantra, vermilion powder and black mustard seeds in the manner I had been told. On a certain Sunday, I gave Masi the sacred object, explaining that she should make an opening in her son's pillow and then insert it. After that, the opening had to be sewn up.

'Leave it in for forty days and make sure that no one else knows about it, not even your husband,' I said.

Her son began a miraculous recovery within the first week and was completely cured of his leprosy by the third week. The sadhu had told me I was allowed to use this singhi only once, and then it was to be immersed in a river or stream. At the end of the prescribed period, I asked Masi to return it to me. She went home and opened up the pillow but there was no singhi to be found.

There could be four explanations for this. One, she took it out but didn't tell me. This was hard to believe as she would not put her son in danger by distorting a tantric talisman. Two, someone else had removed it. Three, it had fallen out. These two options were unlikely because no one else knew about the singhi and it had been carefully sewn into the stuffing of the pillow. Four, it disappeared on its own. I never figured out where it went but it doesn't matter. The fact remains that the boy was cured in a matter of a few days when all other treatments had failed for years. His condition didn't recur.

This encounter with the holy man created more questions than answers. Who was the sadhu? How did he manifest in my dream? Why did he choose me for the singhi? How had he attained knowledge of the occult? Despite the questions, I was awestruck at the experience I had had. And the sadhu had appeared at a time when I really needed divine intervention to give me hope and show me the way forward. This incident served to renew my faith in God.

I began to diligently practise the tantric method in my sadhana. Whenever I heard there was a saint or tantrik in town, I made it a point to visit him or her. At first, they wouldn't take me seriously because I was just a 'child'. But, as I sat there and spoke about my own sadhana, my understanding of astrology, the Vedas and other literature, the look in their eyes would change. They would then give me a proper audience, sharing their own experiences and giving me tips on what I could do differently. However, most of them had no clue about the actual practice or challenges of sadhana. Their knowledge was purely bookish. The genuine sadhaks were in a minority, one in a hundred, but they gave me enough fuel to keep my fire going.

I slipped away at every opportunity to meditate in isolated places, did many yajnas, fire offerings, chanted various mantras and performed sadhanas of yakshinis, yoginis, apsaras and devis, who were all different forms of the tantric feminine energy. But there were virtually no results. No god or celestial being appeared. I began creating my own spiritual practice, borrowing rituals from various sadhanas and using different ingredients and mantras in a way I thought would work for me.

During the month of Kartik (from mid-October to mid-November), I visited a deserted area where a flower called the mandara pushpa grew. I would pluck 108 flowers, come home, make a garland of the flowers and chant over it. Then I'd put it in the fridge. The following morning, I would do a yajna and then go to the Shiva temple to offer the garland to the Shivalingam. This tantric sadhana was supposed to bestow the practitioner with a vision of Shiva. I followed this practice annually for three years from the age of twelve but there were no tangible results.

The frustrating part was that I didn't know where I was going wrong, and there was no one to show me the path. My family members certainly couldn't help me. In fact, they didn't even know what I was up to. They had no idea of the parallel existence of my mystical world or of my deep interest in the occult. They often thought I was in the library when I was actually busy conducting a shastrartha, scriptural colloquy, with some saint or discussing my sadhana with a tantrik. My mother knew of my inclinations but was unaware of the details. Her unconditional support of my quest was a great blessing for me though.

My frustration began to give way to despair. If God existed, why didn't he appear before me? If the scriptures were right, if tantra had any substance, why wasn't I getting the desired outcome? Where was I failing? Though powerful dreams and visions continued and even guided me along my path, I wasn't convinced. I wanted a physical manifestation, real proof that could stand my test of truth.

Gradually, it dawned upon me that I had embarked on a lonely and difficult journey towards self-realization. It would require great tenacity, discipline and time if I wanted to succeed. No matter what spiritual practice I followed, how I did it or how long I did it, there were no guarantees for me. Moving from ephemeral pleasures to a state of constant joy, rising from worldly emotions and being able to live in a state of eternal bliss was going to be a very personal affair. I was my best friend and worst enemy on this journey. I had to create my own way, for the weeds of time had long covered the divine path trod by the ancient sages.

THREE

Stocks and God

The more time I spent in sadhana, the more critical I became of astrology. While astrology merely focused on the twelve signs of the zodiac and the nine planets, my sadhana exposed me to the existence of a vast and infinite inner world. I was beginning to see how I—and everyone around me—was an exact replica of the universe. If there were numerous stars in the universe, the macrocosm, there were countless cells in my body, the microcosm. If there were a sun and moon beyond, there was a solar and lunar channel of breathing within. If there was 70 per cent water on the earth, there was also 70 per cent water in my body.

When innumerable planets, which twinkled like the mysterious stars, were visible to the naked eye, how was I to believe that only nine planets were affecting everyone's lives? And even with these nine planets that astrology considered, I found it odd that Earth was not included. Two planets, Rahu and Ketu, didn't even exist in the solar system, and the moon had the status of a planet when it was really just a satellite. I couldn't come to terms with the notion that Mars, which was millions of miles away, had the ability to influence my life while the very planet that sustained me, where I lived, had no place in the astrological chart.

I felt it was silly to spend time figuring out what the planets had in store for me rather than paying attention to my own actions and their consequences. Instead of creating my own destiny, I was looking up to inanimate revolving balls in the universe to steer me. Nevertheless, I continued to practise astrology because my income from the readings paid for my books and other expenses.

However, I stopped recommending stones and amulets for people to wear for I no longer believed in these remedies. I tried to tell people that they ought to take control of their lives and it was fine to be guided by astrological charts but it was not prudent to live by its predictions. Yet, they wanted to hear that the planets were the cause of their problems, not their own choices. My view was simple: if you keep doing what you've been doing, you'll keep getting what you've been getting.

It is human nature to think that we are merely the subjects and that someone else, perhaps God, is calling the shots. It is convenient to believe that we are being punished or rewarded by divine forces. The truth is that our future is determined by the choices we make today, and our today is resting on the choices we made yesterday.

Most of my clients thought astrological remedies would give them respite from their struggles. They believed that a talisman would manage, somehow, to change negative circumstances into positive ones even if they continued to make poor or harmful choices. People wanted to believe that planetary remedies would sort out their issues and a change in their mindset was not required. I saw that people were not ready to hear my truth. I felt exactly like Nietzsche, who once said, 'They don't understand me: I'm not the mouth for these ears.'

I didn't want lifeless charts and distant planets to dictate the course of *my* life, intrude into my plans and karma. I was determined to script my own future. With my horoscope in one hand and a matchbox in the other, I went to the terrace one day. My brother followed me. Sensing what I was up to, he rushed downstairs to tell our mother that I was turning my horoscope into ashes. Meanwhile, I set the paper on fire. She came up running and rescued the half-burnt horoscope from my hands.

'You shouldn't burn a horoscope, Amit. It must be protected. It is an object of reverence.'

'Ma, there's nothing sacred about a horoscope. I can't revere a piece of paper.'

'A very learned Brahmin had written it when you were born.'

'That doesn't mean anything. Do you really think a horoscope has my destiny already written? Even Rama's horoscope was matched with Sita's. In fact, it was matched by the great sage Vashistha himself, but what happened? He was sent to exile and, later, he even abandoned Sita. Why?'

'I don't have answers to your questions, Amit. What I do know is that just because we don't have the answer to something, it doesn't mean it's false or meaningless. I'm not stopping you from believing what you want but I can't let you burn this horoscope.'

'Ah, don't be upset.' I threw my arms around her and kissed her cheeks several times in quick succession. 'I can write my own horoscope whenever I want.'

'You are very naughty and strong-willed,' she said. 'It doesn't hurt to listen to your elders sometimes, you know. I must go now, I was in the middle of boiling milk. I'll get a new horoscope made and won't give it to you,' she added on her way down.

'Don't waste your money, Ma,' I said, laughing.

Nevertheless, I was confused again. What if my mother was right, what if there was truth to all this and I was the one who couldn't see it? It was true that not everything my horoscope said materialized, but what about the parts where it was completely accurate, where it unerringly predicted many events of my life? I thought hard for a while, weighing the entire matter carefully, examining all aspects of astrology. Finally, I made a clear and firm decision: astrology wasn't going to be a consideration in my life choices.

I had to go beyond astrology because it mostly dealt with the outcome, not the journey. It could predict from a chart whether a person would be a saint or a sinner but it was quiet on how one could go about it. It could show a moment but not the movement leading up to it. My horoscope said that I would achieve self-realization, but it couldn't tell me how.

As I began to move away from astrology, I started focusing more and more on my meditation. At every opportunity, even while riding my bike or bathing, I would build my concentration on the sonic energy in the mantras. But I didn't see God, go into a trance or attain any special powers like the books were saying. Somewhere, I knew I was missing a key element. According to the sacred books, only a guru can guide the disciple and expound on the esoteric aspects of sadhana. While I understood that my journey of self-realization was my responsibility, I realized I needed a guru to help me unravel the mysteries of sadhana; it wasn't going to be easy to find success on my own.

But where to go looking for a guru? I could not think of anyone better than my mother's eldest brother, R.K. Modgil. He was her idol and her ideal. Although he worked as a superintendent in the Indian Railways, this was not his speciality. He was actually an ardent Shiva devotee, and from the age of thirteen till his last breath, he visited the cremation ground twice a day and lit a butter lamp. No one knew what sadhana he did there because he never disclosed it. Like everyone else, all I knew was that he lit a butter lamp. Dogs, birds, cows and other animals followed him there on a daily basis.

My uncle led a simple and truthful life and that is what always inspired me. It was so easy to talk to him; there was no pretence or hyperbole, just plain truth that would pierce my heart. I hoped that if he initiated me, I might start to get some results from my mantra sadhana. But, whenever I asked him, he gently dodged my request. I was not surprised. After all, there was no comparison between the two of us: he, in his fifties, had put in more hours of sadhana than I, at fifteen, had lived altogether.

One day, we happened to be at his place. He had just returned from his morning visit to the cremation ground. 'Come with me,' he said. I followed him, and he took me up to the terrace. I noticed he was holding a tiny, round box in his hands. When he opened it, it turned out to be empty but for a little ash. He pressed his thumb into the ash and then rubbed it against my forehead. 'This is forty years of my tapas,' he said.

I looked at him in wide-eyed surprise.

'I've been consecrating this ash with the same mantra every day for forty years,' he added, 'and you are the first and the last to have it.'

I knelt down in the greatest reverence, for he just initiated me.

'What mantra should I chant?'

'You will be travelling all over the world and I don't want to tie you down by giving you a mantra that you must chant every day. Be free. Go live your dream. No power in the three worlds can stop you.'

He gave me three instructions, principles of life, if you will. Any instruction from a guru to a disciple must remain between them. Only when the disciple becomes someone's guru and wishes to pass on that message are the words uttered again.

That day, he brought his horoscope to me. 'I have just one question,' he said.

I knew his question wasn't going to be an easy one.

'What is the date of my death?'

I was a little shaken. 'Mamaji, 'I can calculate it but my astrologer's code of conduct prohibits me from disclosing such information.'

'I already know my date. I just want to confirm it.'

I couldn't refuse him. His word was my command. We agreed that he would write down the date he knew, and I would do the same on another piece of paper. Then he would give me his slip and I would give him mine. I was curious to find out if he truly knew the date. Mine was a matter of calculation, although deep and intense, but his would be a matter of intuition. Could intuition match the precision of calculation? I took out my notepad and started my calculations based on his horoscope. After an hour, we exchanged slips.

When I read the date he had written, I knew right away that hiding behind his ordinary appearance was an extraordinary consciousness. He had completely mastered his intuitive faculties. Obviously, I never forgot the date and neither did he. Several years later, I would call him from Australia one day before his date of departure from this world. He was in hospital to undergo a minor surgery. Fit and healthy, he had even played basketball before going into the hospital. We were both sentimental over the phone.

'Do you think I will come out of the operation theatre?' he asked.

'Yes, why not? Not only that, you will play basketball again.'

I was happy to lie and I was happy to believe in that lie. At that moment, how dearly I wished for my own prediction and his intuition to go wrong. Mamaji's doctor declared the operation a success, and admitted him into the ICU so he could recover. He did not come out of it alive.

❦

I was nearly fourteen when a scholarly figure, Prof. A.P. Sharma, entered my life. A PhD in English Literature, he had known my father from his college days and had recently moved back to our town after his retirement. An excellent palmist, he read my palm and I his horoscope the very first day we met. We both made predictions about each other and laughed. When two tradesmen of the same trade meet, there is little they can do to impress each other but, in my case, I loved Prof. Sharma from the outset. Cultured and soft-spoken, he was full of warmth.

He lived alone in his old paternal house. Other than the hundreds of books that took up most of the space in the house, his only other possessions were some bookcases, a bed, a sofa, an almirah and a study table. He had piles and piles of notebooks too, full of literary criticism and his musings on life. He adored his books and never left home without locking the bookcases.

I would visit him several times a week and thoroughly enjoyed his company. He would work with me to improve my English-language skills. English literature was his passion, and he would quote Austen, Chaucer, Shakespeare, Keats, Frost, Whitman, Dickens, Hemingway, Wordsworth, Wilde and others without ever opening a book.

He often highlighted passages in his books and scribbled his thoughts along the margins of the pages. Writing in books was something I never appreciated. My philosophy was simple: books were for reading and notebooks were for writing. To me, books were an immaculate work of art and marking in books was like drawing graffiti on a Picasso. You don't spoil what you love.

That said, his love for English literature and language and was infinitely more than I could ever imagine. For me, language was a functional tool, a craft even, to convey what I had in my mind. For him, it was not just a medium of communication but an art through which he created a whole new world. 'When you write, I want the writing to be so taut that if anyone is to remove even a comma from your sentence, the entire paragraph will have to be rewritten. When you speak, I want you to struggle, not because you cannot think of words with which to express yourself but because so many rush to your mind that you have to really choose to pick the word that is most apt, that is perfect,' he said more than once.

One of our favorite pastimes was to sit in the soft winter sun and read classics. I would read and he would peel oranges, carefully removing the pith, putting the pips into a bowl and giving me the juicy segments to eat. During those hours spent in the sunshine, he often read my palm and made remarkably accurate predictions. We also talked a great deal about other things. There were no restraints or rules in our conversations, and my age was not a bar.

'Why don't you tell me about your girlfriends?' he asked once.

'Girlfriends? I don't have any.'

'I don't believe you!'

'I'm telling you the truth, Uncle.'

'How can this be? You are young and expressive. You get good grades and the whole school knows you because of your astrology. Some girl must have a crush on you or you must be attracted to someone.'

'But it's true; I don't have anyone.' I felt rather shy having this conversation with him. 'The religious texts say that until one is twenty-five years old, one should be a brahmachari.'

'This is old school. You must live your life, you must enjoy it. All our sages had consorts.'

'No, I think the ancient books have some truth to them. Besides, who has the time for a girlfriend? When will I do my reading, play chess, practise astrology or play the keyboard if I start devoting time to a girlfriend?'

'Oh, you are so uptight, Amit. Why are you so rigid? Loosen up a bit.'

'How will I spend time with you if I have a girlfriend?'

'You are all head and no heart. Never mind, one day you'll fall head over heels for some girl and won't be able to live without her.'

'That will never happen, I know myself. I won't marry.'

'Your palm says it loud and clear. The line of marriage is pink, unbroken and strong. You will be married before you turn twenty-eight.'

'I don't think so.'

'What is wrong with you? You scare me with your ascetical and religious bent.'

You are all head and no heart. This became his standard line. This was how many conversations would end when he was unable to discern an emotional side to me. The truth was that in spite of my trying, I couldn't feel any attachment. I did not miss anything or anyone, not even Prof. Sharma. I tried mixing with friends, with other people, but I found little joy in these associations. I wasn't doing this deliberately; this was just the way I was. On this particular occasion when he spoke about my marriage with such conviction, I did wonder if he was right about my life. It was true that both my palm and my horoscope predicted marriage. Was I really in control of some preordained destiny? I thought about this for a while, and then decided I wasn't going to let a certain line on my palm dictate my future for me. I was determined to write the script of my own life.

Engrossed in my thoughts and a little agitated, I left Prof. Sharma's house without saying goodbye. When I reached home, I found my mother sitting by the altar reading a sacred text as usual. That evening, she was studying the *Bhagavat Purana*, the epic narrating the glories of Lord Krishna. Rather than giving her the usual peck, I just sat down near her.

'You know, Mum,' I said, 'I can be whatever you want me to be—a high-ranking official, businessman or professor. I only have one request: please do not force me or expect me to get married. I want to give my life to a spiritual cause. No one believes me when I tell them I will not get married.'

She could have easily brushed off my thoughts, dismissing my request as a teenager's idealism. Instead, she said, 'I believe you. You are free to lead your life the way you please. I will never bind you to something you don't like, Amit. We can revisit this when you grow a bit older though. Who knows, you may have a change of heart. Why don't you want to marry, anyway?'

I replied, 'I have seen more than three thousand horoscopes. Everyone has similar problems. What are they doing? They are born, they go to school and college, get a job, get married, have kids, go through the grind, become old and die. After hearing the problems of married people, I can categorize them into two types. The first involves people who are unable to make their marriage work. Though they have been married for quite a while, each day is a drag and they part ways eventually. Then you have the ones who are trying hard to make it work. Even for them, most days are tiring, but in between disagreements and confrontations, between the arguments and bickering, they also have good moments.

All in all, it's too much work. Most people get married because they feel the need to do so, but I don't. More importantly, marriage plays no role in my path. Instead, I wish to do penance in the woods like the legendary Dhruva, like our sages of ancient times. I want to see if God really exists.'

'If?' she said in surprise. 'Why do you do various sadhanas now if you still doubt God's existence?'

'I do sadhana because I want to see him, Ma. I want to meet my creator. I believe he exists but how can I be sure until I see him? I doubt his existence sometimes because if he really exists, why is there suffering and misery in the world? If there's one God, why are there so many religions? Why did he allow it?'

'Faith, child. Faith erases all questions.'

'I wish! Faith does not erase questions. It only ignores or discourages them.'

'I know I can't win this debate with you. I just know that God is real. He protects, provides and is watching over us.'

I wanted to continue but there was a knock on the front door. It was Prof. Sharma. He had come to check on me, thinking he had upset me. I was only too happy to see him again. He had brought mangoes as a peace offering.

For reasons I never quite understood, he loved me deeply. He had two photos of me in his wallet. Each time I got a passport picture clicked, he insisted on having one. The latest photo would go in his wallet and he would use the older one as a bookmark. He would make tea for me and serve it in an exquisite bone-china cup and saucer that he wouldn't allow anyone else to touch.

I had nothing to offer him, yet every gesture of his was full of care and love for me. 'I'm at the twilight of my life, Amit,' he would often say after a drink. 'I won't be there to see you grow and conquer the world, or partake of your success. I wish I had not been born so early.'

His eyes would well up.

'But can you promise me something?'

'Yes, Uncle. Anything for you.'

'When I die, I would just like you to be by my side. I would like to hold your hand in mine and breathe my last.'

I assured him I would be there for him without knowing if it would happen that way. It didn't. I gave him that reassurance because he was looking for it. But, thinking about his death, I didn't feel any pain of separation. Maybe he was right after all: I was all reason and he was all feeling.

⁂

Once, there were floods in our region. From the roof, you could see animals, furniture, utensils and many other unidentifiable objects floating down the streets. When the flood waters ebbed after some days and we entered our house, the most terrible thing was to see my books dead. They were swollen exactly like corpses and lay soiled and defaced. I put them in the sunlight, hoping to dry them, but the pages just curled in the heat. And they stank. Left with the memory of what they had been, I couldn't bear looking at them anymore. I didn't want to sell them to the scrap dealer, for you don't sell love. On a sunny day devoid of wind, I took them to the terrace and cremated them. All of them. Then I picked myself up and moved on.

Meanwhile, my parents decided to build a room on the first floor of the house so that we would have shelter should such a situation arise again in the future. The vendor who supplied us the building material was a man in his mid-thirties called Parvesh Singla. The first time I visited his shop, we had a casual conversation and connected immediately. After that, we began meeting frequently.

Like Prof. Sharma, he cared about me deeply. Once again, I could not quite comprehend why. I was unable to understand why a successful businessman like him hung out with a teenager like me.

I asked, 'Why do you spend so much of your time with me? You buy books and pens for me, you take me out for dinners. Why?'

'I don't know what draws me to you, but you have this pull, Amit. You seem to have no confusion of any sort. And I always wanted a brother like you,' he replied.

I sat there thinking he was being sentimental like Prof. Sharma. I also felt guilty because I didn't feel any attachment for him. For me, he was a good human being I cared about, and we had common interests. We discussed philosophical issues and shared business ideas with each other. Astute at creating wealth, Parvesh had built multiple sources of income for himself.

On one occasion, he said, 'I earn from my businesses but I grow my wealth through stocks.'

'Wow! Will you teach me how to invest in stocks? I have money left over from my astrological readings, and would like to invest somewhere.'

'Yes, I'll teach you, but remember you can only gain if you are prepared to lose.'

He showed me how he picked stocks. He only invested in the primary market—in IPOs—as he believed they were safer.

'Never love your stocks. Never forget that you buy them to make a profit. Once you have reached a profitable position, exit. If they betray you and you are making a loss, exit. Your goal is to make more profits than losses.'

I took a plunge in the financial world. I read voraciously, studying all the financial publications I could get my hands on. Over the next few months, I started buying stocks through sub-brokers. I also enjoyed and actively traded in the secondary markets; they were faster, riskier, more fun. 90 per cent of my savings were now invested in shares. Stock trading was dangerous and exciting. I could lose all my savings or multiply them with little effort. Whenever stock prices shot up, I was delighted, and whenever they went down, I felt a sense of loss. I enjoyed riding this roller coaster of emotions.

I passed class ten at the age of fifteen, scored 80 per cent and secured a place in the college of my choice. I chose to study commerce because, after my interest in the occult, it was business that fascinated me. I liked business because I liked challenge. On the one hand, I had seen the staid work routine of my parents, who went to work and came back at the same time every day. On the other, I saw Parvesh's exciting rise in the world of commerce. His thrilling account of the ups and downs of his business was more fascinating than Prof. Sharma reminiscing about his college days. It was just a matter of temperament and, given mine, I was more inclined towards the former.

Seeing my passion for business, everyone around me thought I was obsessed about money. I did enjoy entrepreneurship and making money, and financial independence was certainly a good thing. Yet, there was a deeper reason why I focused on business and continued with astrology even though I'd understood it wasn't going to give me the answers I sought. By now, I knew without the shadow of a doubt that I wanted to give up the material world and walk the spiritual path. My hunger for God was stronger than anything else within me. Innumerable times, I'd thought of renouncing the world and going to the Himalayas to do austere penance. It was the soft eyes of my mother and her loving voice that always held me back. I didn't think she would be able to bear the separation. Worldly activities helped me curb my inner desire and pull on. I did not know how else to channelize my energies or distract myself.

Whatever I tried my hand at though, I mastered almost effortlessly. Soon, it would cease to challenge me. Whether it was learning chess or playing a musical instrument, singing Vedic hymns or practising astrology, each activity stopped stimulating me after a while. I wanted a task to really engage me, test me, surprise me, but everything felt so easy.

Looking for something new, I decided to enroll in an advanced computer course at a private institution. At the end of the orientation on the first day, a young man wearing a turban and rather shabby clothes came up to me. I actually thought he was a motor mechanic because there were small stains that looked like oil or grease smears on his clothes.

Introducing himself as Harpreet Singh, he posed a question on the Bhagavadgita.

I don't know why he asked me a religious question. I normally applied a tilak on my forehead, but hadn't done so that day. I was dressed in jeans and a T-shirt, which is what I normally wore. He had no idea I practised astrology or that I had studied many religious texts, yet he chose to ask me a question on the Bhagavadgita in a computer centre. Anyhow, the question was not outside my field of knowledge.

As I finished answering him, he suddenly asked, 'Where did you learn English?'

'How weird!' I thought. Rather than focusing on my answer, he only saw the language I used. Anyway, we chatted for a while. I told him I was doing that advanced computer course in order to build an application for the financial markets.

'Financial markets?'

'Yeah, I trade in both the primary and secondary market. And I want to code an investment monitoring tool.'

'Are you free for a few hours?' he said.

'Umm ... now? Okay, but what do you do?'

'Have you heard of *Chardikala*?'

'Of course.' *Chardikala* was a regional newspaper in the Punjabi language.

'I work there.'

Harpreet Singh took me to his office. He drove his scooter while I followed him on my moped. When we walked into the office, he took me into a cabin. The sign on the door said 'Chief Editor and Publisher'. He turned on the air conditioning, picked up the phone and asked for someone. A man came in and my new friend ordered some tea. I was curious now.

'Who are you? And how come you are in the chief editor's cabin?'

He smiled. 'This is us,' he said pointing to a family picture on the desk.

'What do you mean?'

'Harpreet Singh Dardi. That's my full name. My father owns this enterprise.'

'Oh really!'

'Now, tell me something,' he said. 'Would you like to write for our newspaper?'

'I've never written for any newspaper. And I don't write in Punjabi. Also, what could I possibly write on?'

'We launched an English language financial publication last year called *The Business Times* and it's doing well. I'm looking for a good columnist.'

And so it happened that I began writing a regular column for them with my stock picks. Pleased with my work, a few months later, they offered me the role of editor to run their weekly edition. I readily accepted. Soon, I was spending most evenings at the press. Writing editorials, selecting news items and editing the work of other journalists gave me an intellectual kick.

A couple of years later, I resigned and moved on to grow my part-time business of making computerized presentations for small businesses. My stint at the press came in handy while writing content. After finishing class twelve, I stopped going to junior college and opted for distance education so I could better utilize my time. My college education had completely disappointed me, and I couldn't see what I had learned in the past two years. I thought of studying abroad, but affordability was a big issue. I didn't have any siyar singhi I could use to fulfil my ambition to go abroad. But I did have a mantra with me. It was said that chanting this mantra would send the practitioner on a voyage. Its sonic vibrations were supposed to manifest your desire—the law of attraction.

I expressed my desire to the Universe and started chanting the mantra in January 1998. While driving, bathing, eating, travelling, before sleeping, upon getting up, day and night when I wasn't doing anything else, I meditated on the mantra with great mindfulness. I had faith in the mantra but I wasn't sure if it would work quickly enough. My scepticism disappeared one day in March when one of my acquaintances casually mentioned her cousin, who was an education consultant and sent students to Australia.

I asked my father, and he immediately approved of the idea of my higher education in Australia. I enrolled in a two-year diploma in information technology at Hurstville Business College in Sydney. My father made withdrawals from his retirement fund to pay for the first year's college fee and my air ticket. I used my savings to do some shopping and buy Australian dollars. Meanwhile, I left behind my shares as a long-term investment.

If I thought India was hard work for me, I didn't know what lay ahead in Australia. I had no tertiary degrees and no relevant work experience to help me settle down in a new country and be able to earn enough to support myself. I didn't even have full working rights since I could only work twenty hours per week on a student visa. What was to become of me? What chance did I really have? I just had the willingness to work hard, very hard.

At eighteen, I was on my way to Australia. Chanting the mantra had manifested my desire, but I was responsible for living through the consequences. Alone but overconfident, unprepared but resolute, clueless but hopeful at heart, I was ready to face everything life would throw at me.

FOUR

First Flight

I distinctly remember feeling numb on two occasions in my life. The first was when I was flying to Australia and the second was twelve years later when I took renunciation. No, this was not a physical numbness but a sort of emotional paralysis. I remember not feeling any emotions. My family, along with a couple of family friends, came to see me off at the airport. Though they didn't say much, their eyes spoke volumes. I was going to a place thousands of miles away without knowing when I would return.

No one in the family had ever been on a plane before, let alone leave the country altogether. At the airport, they talked about everything else except my impending departure. This wasn't something they wanted to think about because, on the train of thoughts about my future, the only passengers were worries, insecurities and the pain of separation. I remember saying goodbye as I passed through the security barrier. My loved ones stood watching me. I looked hopeful and helpless while they looked sad and helpless.

The flight from New Delhi to Sydney was a little adventure for me. It was not like the first sighting of the bookshop when I was five or like my first trip to the library. Those were pleasant and joyful discoveries and there had been no confusion at all. Here, I was doing things I'd never done before, like working out the mechanics of the seat belt and trying to understand what the paper bag was for. I didn't know if they charged for meals and drinks or what was stocked in the tiny restroom. Above all, I didn't know what awaited me in Australia.

Thoughts of the future—nice and not so nice—continued to bubble in my mind. I wasn't anxious or nervous though; internally, I was prepared to handle whatever came my way. I was simply quiet. This had always been my way. In the face of grave adversity, extreme joy or an unfamiliar emotion, I would become quiet. The quietude allowed the emotion I was experiencing to sink in and it allowed me to think. I held no conversations with my fellow passengers; I didn't watch any movies or listen to music. I simply sat there, dreaming and reflecting.

I remembered how excited I had been when my agent, who had not only handled my college admission but also my travel arrangements, had told me that my college would be arranging for a 'home stay': I would be living with an Australian family. This kind of accommodation would give me a chance to learn about Australian culture. I was also pleased to know that vegetarian food wouldn't be an issue for the family.

'We've already sent the fax to the college administration and they'll arrange for someone,' the agent told me. 'They will hold a placard with your name on it at the airport,' he said with conviction.

Upon my arrival in Sydney, I went through immigration and baggage collection and then waited in the arrivals area. I was eager to see who was coming to pick me up and wondered what kind of family I would be staying with. I waited and waited but no one turned up. I approached the crowd outside, scanning people's faces anxiously, expecting someone to step forward and ask if I was Amit Sharma. I peered at the signs they were holding, hoping my name might be on one of them. I went from one corner of the arrivals area to the other, thinking I may have come out of the wrong exit. But my efforts were in vain.

I passed an hour moving around like a squirrel searching for walnuts in the rainy season. I was slightly nervous and restless; hopeful too. The faces of my loved ones flashed before me. They must have been wondering if I'd reached safely. I got change for five dollars from a florist at the airport. Popping two one-dollar coins into a payphone, I made a brief call home to let them know I was safe and sound and everything was fine. My family was relieved to hear my voice.

I went back to waiting, which I did for another three hours. Anyone who could have turned up or intended to be here should have been here by now, I thought. Eventually, I concluded that no one was coming to get me. Later, the college administration would tell me that they were never given any intimation about an airport pick up or a home stay arrangement.

Now, I had nowhere to go. Other than the Australian flag, kangaroos and the Sydney Opera House, all of which I had seen on the TV and on the college brochure, I recognized nothing else in Australia. I knew no one here. Actually, that wasn't entirely true. I did have a cousin here but I wasn't in touch with him.

A friend of a friend lived in Australia as well. I had a number for him, in fact, two numbers. I tried them but both turned out wrong numbers. For a moment, I felt a sweat break out on my body. I scratched my head. Literally. Where was I to go now? Where could I find a place to stay and where would I eat? I could go to a hotel but, with just over three thousand dollars being my entire lifeline, how long could I survive?

Just then, I remembered that my agent's son lived in Sydney, and he had given me his son's phone number. 'You can call him if there's any emergency,' he had said. Well, this was an emergency for me. I tried the number. Someone picked up the phone; it was the agent's son. I thanked my lucky stars. I briefly told him about the home stay fiasco and that I had nowhere to go.

'My brother and sister have gone to India for the next three weeks, so I can accommodate you,' he said. 'Take a taxi and come over.' He gave me his address.

I hailed a taxi and got in. The taxi driver said, 'G'day mate.' I had no clue what he said because it didn't sound like English to me. I'd never come across an Australian accent, not even in the Hollywood movies I had seen. Besides, I hadn't watched that many. Maybe twenty in all, ranging from *Baby's Day Out* to *The Terminator*.

I gave the address and we were on our way. My, my, how spic and span everything was. I never thought such cleanliness and organization were even possible. Finally, we arrived at our destination—Falcon Street in North Sydney. I don't remember the house number. The weather was cold: I had arrived on 21 June. Fortunately, it was a Sunday. Had it been a weekday, the agent's son would not have been home and no one would have taken my call. Meanwhile, after paying for the cab and phone calls, I was down by $36. Nearly 1 per cent of my savings was already gone.

I dragged my heavy bags to the first floor. My host, a young man in his early twenties, introduced himself as Happy. He asked me to leave my bags in the living room. It was a one-bedroom apartment.

'You can sleep on the sofa bed,' he offered.

I nodded. I was just glad to be somewhere with a roof over my head.

Happy had another friend over for the weekend. A postgraduate in commerce, he was there on a student visa and worked in a factory. Soon, four other guys joined us. They all worked in the same factory and one of them had recently got his taxi driver's licence.

The postgraduate gave me some unsolicited advice as we were sitting around: 'If you think you can get a job, forget it. I have an MCom from Delhi University and I work in a factory here. There's too much racism in this country and Indian degrees or experience have no value. Local work experience is all that matters.'

'Can't he get a security guard's licence?' another fellow asked.

'The course costs around $1,200, if he can afford it, but even after that, he may or may not get any shifts, as you know,' the master of commerce proclaimed like an oracle.

'Yeah. Perhaps he can get a job at a car wash.'

'Maybe.'

'As a waiter at a restaurant?'

'He wouldn't understand their accent.'

'Can he work in a countryside farm?'

'He can do that if he doesn't get anything else. It's not ideal because he won't be able to study that way. He can go to the farms if he doesn't pass his exams or if his visa runs out. I know someone who can offer him a job; he has a potato farm.' This was Mr Commerce again.

'Taxi driver?'

'You're kidding me! You have to memorize all the street names and routes. Do you know how difficult the test for the licence is?'

Till now, I had not participated in the discussion. This was going on between them quite independently of me. Ordinarily, I couldn't have cared about what they said or thought about me. I didn't have to prove myself to anybody, and certainly not to these people. However, looking at their zest and concern for me, I feared they might never stop this conversation.

'Listen folks,' I interrupted. 'I know exactly what I'm here to do and it's not driving taxis, washing cars or ripping potatoes. Before I run out of money, I'll have something more fitting arranged for me.' I said some more things that I can't recall now, but I do remember speaking for about five minutes non-stop. They didn't bother me after that.

Happy asked me to pay rent from the very first day I arrived. 'The phone bill will be on actuals, the utilities on a pro rata basis,' he added. And I had to find my own accommodation within three weeks. Fair enough. But, for now, I was hungry, not having eaten anything since morning. It was well past the lunch hour and no one mentioned lunch. Finally, at about 5 p.m., they got beer and other liquor, and ordered food. They offered me some beer and even insisted that I tried whisky. I refused. Drinking, smoking and partying weren't my style. Besides, I was unfamiliar with these guys. Prof. Sharma and Parvesh were the only two people I knew who drank alcohol. Parvesh drank rather rarely and Prof. Sharma drank extremely gracefully.

All our pleasures live in the brain anyway. I had experienced far better, long-lasting stimulants for my gratification, and they were free of any damaging side effects. An intellectual challenge gave me the greatest thrill. For hours at a stretch, I could happily sit and solve a coding problem or stare at the chessboard, not to mention reading or creating music on my keyboard. Heck, I even got a hangover when a great book ended or I cracked a piece of code.

Above all, there were the joys I knew within. I had experienced the pleasure of diving into the ocean of meditation. I had felt the rapture of chanting Vedic verses, where each escalating sound would transport me to another world. If there was adrenalin for the soul, if there was an intoxicant of the spirit, for me, it was meditation.

The next morning, I walked to the bank to start a new account. The bank manager was friendly and greeted me with a big smile. No one jumped the line; the place was well organized but relaxed. In less than thirty minutes, I had a bank account number and a temporary ATM card. On my way back home, I picked up a free local newspaper. It was full of advertisements seeking administrative secretaries, assistants, telemarketers and so on. There were no jobs for programmers, editors or salespeople though. I found out later that only mainstream newspapers advertised the types of jobs I was searching for.

In the afternoon, I went to my new college. It was just a few rooms occupying one floor in a small building. The principal, Richard Da Silva, was a nice man. I introduced myself and requested him to help me find a job, but he said there was nothing he could do. I asked him if he could help me get work experience without pay, and he promised to try.

Close to the flat, I found a business centre where I could prepare, print and fax my *résumé* to companies. I applied for numerous secretarial and administrative jobs. After spending about an hour sending faxes, I rushed home to be close to the phone in case anyone called. I sat by the phone the entire day but it didn't ring. Day two: I sent out more faxes. Day three: I learned that I had to make follow-up calls to the recruitment consultants at the various companies; they wouldn't call me.

Day four: I called home and let them know all was well. It turned out my mother had spoken to her elder brother whose son, Arun Modgil, lived in Sydney. He had suggested I contact my cousin, which I did. Arun told me he would pick me up on the weekend, and I should pack my things for a couple of days with them. I was glad to be spending some time with Arun and his family.

Day five: I saw not one but two letters in the mail; they had logos printed on them. I was thrilled. Finally, I had got an interview call or maybe even a straight job offer. The first letter turned out to be a polite rejection. It was so courteously worded that I thought they really loved me but couldn't hire me for some genuine reason. I opened the second letter; it sounded just like the first one. I was disappointed, but still appreciated the communication: someone had cared to write that they didn't want me. Nevertheless, I called the numbers printed on the letters and was told that they would let me know if there were any future opportunities.

Normally, in India, I would have shared my experience with someone in the family or with Prof. Sharma, but there was no one here to talk to. Suddenly, I felt a great vacuum. It dawned on me for the first time that I was in a totally new country, all alone. I had no backup and had to find a way to survive. I had to study in college, find work, foot my living expenses as well as save enough to pay for my next year's tuition fees, failing which I could be deported. I went into the bathroom, the only place in Happy's apartment where I had any privacy. Looking into the mirror, I saw that I was crying. I didn't stop myself but let myself go. This was the first and the only time I cried in Australia.

Afterwards, my eyes were puffy and my face looked tired but I felt fresh and light. Perhaps it had just sunk in that I was on my own here and this acceptance had made me feel lighter. Anyhow, I couldn't afford to look scruffy because I was going to see Arun in less than an hour's time and didn't want him to know I had been crying. I washed up and waited for him, my bag packed for the weekend.

He called me from his phone as he approached my flat. I went down quickly. There he was, a handsome man standing beside a sleek Honda Legend. We shook hands and I touched his feet. I had met him only twice earlier, once as a child and another time when he had visited India a few years ago. Sitting beside him as he drove, I was impressed by the car, its squeaky clean, plush leather interiors, automatic transmission and ample leg room.

Arun wasn't keen on students coming on a student visa and then struggling to live and study. He had expressed this some years ago when my mother had consulted him about sending my brother overseas for higher education. He held the opinion that it was better to study well in India and then work abroad if one wanted. It was the reason I had not informed him about my coming to Australia.

'Now that you are here, let's make it work,' he said after I filled him in on my situation.

As we drove, I learnt that Arun had recently quit his job and started a new business in shrink-wrap packaging. An engineer by profession and a genius by design, he would later grow his business into a multimillion-dollar enterprise, with operations in more than ten countries.

Arun lived in Seven Hills, a suburb in the western part of Sydney, quite far from my college. It took us a while to reach his house. When we arrived, he introduced me to his little daughters, Ananta and Ayesha, who were six and three respectively. His wife, Anju, was a certified accountant and worked for a global investment bank. She was at work when I arrived.

Later that evening, she came home. Walking into the living room where Arun and I sat chatting, she tilted her head to one side, gave me a broad smile and said, 'Hello!' Her warmth suddenly made things very easy. She turned out to be a bright and wonderful person, full of love.

Even though it had only been a week since I had left India, it felt like an eternity. Within this one week, I had reported at college, got my medical insurance and a new bank account, applied for at least twenty jobs, got two written rejections, scoured the streets of north Sydney, gone for a sales seminar thinking it was an interview call, been interviewed for the job of a chess tutor, applied for work experience at the college and become comfortable with the Australian accent. I was also down by more than two hundred dollars.

On Saturday, Arun and Anju had some friends over. Unlike the young men earlier, this was a sober crowd. We had an enjoyable dinner and I played a few songs on the Yamaha keyboard I'd brought from India, while everyone sat back and enjoyed the music. The next day, it was time for me to go back. In the morning, Arun came up to me and said, 'We would like it if you stayed with us till you settled down a bit.'

'I would love it, Bhaiya,' I said, 'but I don't want to be a burden. Is everyone else in the family okay with it?'

'Yeah, I've discussed it with Anju. In fact, this is her idea.'

I was deeply touched at this gesture. Arun kindly offered me the use of his phone line, which had a separate fax machine. As I sat down to send out job applications, my mind was flooded with business ideas; I saw opportunities everywhere. Not wanting to waste any time, I even registered a business name: Webcomm Technologies. The Internet was turning into a massive phenomenon, a juggernaut of possibilities, and I didn't want to miss the boat. The only limitation was that I had no capital to start anything. Having said that, I didn't require a million dollars or even ten thousand. I just needed someone to say, 'Don't worry about the five thousand for next year's college fees and don't worry about food and living for the next six months,' and I would have thrown myself into building a business. However, I didn't have this kind of breathing space at the moment.

I soon discovered that there weren't enough software job openings in the local newspapers and no one was prepared to give me work because I had no local experience. To get in touch with more companies, I would pick up the Yellow Pages every day and call fifty potential employers. I would have even called a hundred but Arun had a quota of a certain number of free local calls from his landline, and I didn't want to exceed that. Once, I called someone who heard me out and said, 'I just felt I was listening to a robot.'

Robot? I had obviously failed. Here I was, trying my hardest, and the fact that the person at the other end thought I was a robot could only mean I was sounding like a machine. What he said next corrected my view. 'I don't have any IT requirements, mate,' he said, 'but would you like to come work for me? I need someone who sounds like you over the phone.'

This was the first compliment I had received from an Australian. I was still hopeful of finding a job in programming, so I politely refused.

With every passing day, however, I was getting increasingly desperate. A week later, I got a telemarketing job offer and snapped it up. This company was based out of a suburb called Baulkham Hills, and it was literally a 'home business': the employer had converted his house into an office. My remuneration was set at $12 an hour plus commission, and I couldn't resist calculating what I would do with that money; it felt like a lot of money all of a sudden.

My job was to pitch our services to small businesses. Once the customer was interested, we would fax them an order form and the deal was done if they signed and faxed back with their credit card details. My employer, an elderly man, had a specific process though. You had to make calls from 9 a.m. till 1 p.m., send faxes in the afternoon and follow up on the phone either in the evening or the next day.

I did not break for lunch or tea. I just called and called. I found out that other telemarketers would manage to get one or two customers interested in the morning. On the very first day, I had over eight such customers in the morning and fourteen in the afternoon session because I made fresh sales calls all day. As soon as I had a customer interested, I ran to the fax machine, sent them a fax and made an immediate follow-up call so I could close the deal. The first day, I bagged six customers. Wow, I thought.

The boss had a different opinion. He did not appreciate my faxing at unscheduled hours. 'You have to follow the process,' he told me the next day. 'We only send faxes during the lunch hour.' I apologized and went back to making calls at my desk. I had nearly thirty keen customers but no deal closures on the second day. As far as I was concerned, you had to strike when the iron was hot. It was simple, a no-brainer.

The third day, I sought the help of the operations manager, an older lady who reported to the boss. I explained to her that I could exceed all my targets provided I was allowed to send faxes right away. She took up my request with him while I waited outside his cabin. After a few minutes, he came out with her and said in my presence, 'Tell this idiot to get outta here.'

I had never been spoken about in this way. I needed money, sure, but I wasn't prepared to be insulted. Like they say, there's always a first time; this was my first time, and I had been caught off guard.

'Watch your language, man,' I said.

'F**k you,' he replied.

I stood there stunned. The lady hastily asked me to leave as the old man could get quite mad.

'Are you going to pay me wages and commission for two days or not?' I asked the lady.

'Get the f**k outta here,' he answered on her behalf.

'What's wrong with you, man?' I said. Feeling helpless, I tried to match his pitch and authority but couldn't. I sounded meek and insignificant, even to myself. He shook his head and went back in his cabin. The lady urged me to leave.

I picked up my bag and walked out. Deeply stressed and lost in thought, I passed the bus stop without realizing and kept walking. Finally, I collapsed on the kerb. For a long time, I just sat there thinking. My tuition fees of $5,000 were due in about ten months. And I needed to move out of my cousin's house soon. I *had* to find a way to earn my living.

Arun was home when I got back. 'You're back early!' he said affectionately.

'The man swore at me.'

'Who swore?'

'The owner of the company. He swore at me.' I divulged some details.

'That's unusual. But why? What did you do then?'

What could I do? It's not like I had a choice. They asked me to leave.'

'That's awful, but don't worry. You'll find something else,' he said. 'Did they at least pay you for two days of work?'

'They only paid in insults. No cash. I put my pride aside and asked them for my wages but they refused.'

'Screw them. Come on, let's have a coffee.'

He tried to motivate me and make me laugh but I was really dispirited. I didn't feel like doing anything at this point but that wasn't a luxury I could afford. My survival depended on action. I picked up the Yellow Pages and began calling companies with even greater vigour.

Six weeks and fifteen hundred calls later, I got my first opportunity with a company called Australian Windows Publishing (AWP). A lady called Margo Plowright called me for an interview for unpaid work experience in software programming. I went to meet her the next day, and found that she ran that business with her husband.

Unpaid work was not the best offer, of course, as I desperately needed money. But an opportunity to work in the IT industry mattered more to me than a paid opportunity in any other industry. I asked them if I would get to code in C++, a programming language I knew really well, and they indicated I would. The programming language they used was Delphi though, a language I'd never heard of. I wasn't really keen on working in it because there was no growth or future as a Delphi coder. Still, getting any break right now was good enough for me.

AWP offered me four weeks of work experience. The entire time, I was simply copying and renaming HTML files. That was my job. Easy, very easy. I wasn't looking for an easy job though. I had understood quite early in my life that the amount of money you made was directly proportional to the degree of difficulty you could handle. The more stress you could handle, the more money you were paid; easy jobs paid less. Anyhow, I had no choice.

At the beginning of the fourth week, the couple gave me amazing news. 'We're very happy with your work. We would be pleased to offer you a one-year contract. Starting next week, we'll pay you $15 an hour for forty hours a week.'

I couldn't believe my ears. Finally, I had a job offer. Someone thought what I did had value. Money can make you feel important, and I felt important. I thanked them for their offer though I wasn't entirely satisfied. One reason was that I wasn't coding; I was doing something that even a sixth-grader could do. Two, I hadn't yet told my employers that I was allowed only twenty hours paid work per week as stipulated on my student visa.

That evening, while I was attending classes at college, my principal called me into his office. 'Congratulations, Amit, I've got some good news,' he said. We've lined up an interview for you with a software company.'

'Thank you so much, Richard!'

'It's unpaid work experience for two weeks. If they like your work, they may extend it by another two weeks.'

'Awesome!'

'Your interview is on Wednesday.'

On Wednesday, I called in sick at AWP. They didn't mind; I was doing free work after all. I went for my interview with Trading Technology Australia (TTA). This was a small financial software company based downtown. The directors of the company, Gregory Rostron and Joe Maisano, interviewed me. Greg was a Swiss-German who had moved to Australia a long time ago. Joe was of Italian descent but born and raised in Australia.

After the interview, they offered me the position of a computer programmer. I double-checked that my work experience was going to be in programming, and was assured it was. I asked if I would get to code in C++, and they said that C++ was what they generally used. Though I wasn't going to be paid for this work, I was offered a weekly railway pass.

Now, I was faced with a great dilemma. On the one hand, I had a full-time job offer from AWP and they were ready to pay me, but there was no growth or intellectual challenge. On the other hand, TTA was offering an unpaid opportunity for just two weeks with no guaranteed prospects, but the work was in programming, my area of focus and ambition. If I chose TTA, I could be back to square one in a couple of weeks, calling companies for work experience. With AWP, I could still be copying and pasting files a year later. 'What's the worst that can happen?' I asked myself.

FIVE

$15 to $250,000

I reported at the Trading Technology Australia office on Monday. After introducing me to the small team of developers, Joe gave me my first assignment and asked me to build a contact management software.

'A contact management software?' I was a little surprised at this instruction because I thought I was going to work on their financial software.

'Yes, I need an application to manage my list of prospective and existing customers.'

He took me to a computer. 'We have VB loaded on this machine.'

'VB?'

'Yes. Don't you know Visual Basic?'

I had made it clear in the interview that I only knew C++.

'Umm, I don't, but I can try and learn.'

That was that. I sat staring at the screen, not knowing what to do. My computer wasn't connected to the Internet, which meant I couldn't access any reference material from the web to guide me. I knew that if I couldn't code the system, I would be shown the door at the end of two weeks, if not earlier.

The easy job scene at AWP kept intruding into my thoughts, but I was here now, and had to quickly find a solution. I was already down to my last six hundred dollars. At lunchtime, I went out and bought a book on Visual Basic. Four days later, I showed him the full version of my contact management software.

'This is good, mate,' Joe said. 'How come you said you didn't know VB?'

'I didn't really.'

'And you coded this entire software in four days?'

'Well, yes.'

'I'd heard Indians are great programmers . Four days! Amazing.'

'Thanks, Joe. I still need to make many improvements. It's the first version.'

'Go for it, mate.'

He looked at Greg, raised four fingers and said, 'Four days!'

The following Thursday, they extended my work experience for two more weeks.

By the third week at TTA, Greg and Joe had gained enough confidence in me to assign me their flagship product called Ringer. Designed for the financial markets, Ringer was a highly complex and sophisticated piece of software that allowed bonds, forex and options traders to buy and sell based on market movements. Working with a small team of developers, my task was software maintenance. Towards the end of my month there, they offered me a permanent part-time job at $15 an hour—twenty hours a week as per my visa conditions.

I wanted to work more than twenty hours though, but without violating my visa. I approached Greg and Joe.

'It's fine if you pay me for only twenty hours but I would really like to learn more. Can I work here for forty hours a week or longer? I don't have my own computer at home as yet.'

'That's fine,' Greg said. 'We'll give you the office keys and you can leave late if you like.'

I had to work harder, learn quicker and earn more because this was the only way I would ever be able to fulfil the dream I had of studying at university one day. I knew it was a wild dream for it was beyond my range of affordability. My current worry was my college fee because the next instalment—$5,000—would be due in seven months, and I had no clue how I was going to save that sum. I was already working as hard as I reasonably could.

My day usually started at 5 a.m. so that I could take a bath before everyone else. This was to avoid disturbing them later as there was only one bathroom in Arun's house. Once I was ready, I would have a cup of tea with two slices of bread and pack my lunch. This generally consisted of food I had saved up from the night before, or another four slices of bread with jam.

I used to leave home around 6 a.m. and walk 2 km to the station. It was a hilly area and would take me exactly eighteen minutes of brisk walking to reach the train station. Occasionally, Anju gave me a lift to the station when she left early or I left late. It was a forty-five-minute ride to the city and a fifteen-minute walk before I reached the TTA office. I started work at 7:30 a.m. and coded till just after 5 p.m.

From work, it was a twenty-minute train ride to my college, where I would study till 9 p.m. By the time I got back home, it would be nearly 11 p.m. After entering the house quietly since everyone was asleep at that time, I would freshen up and change. Sometimes, I wanted to step into the shower but eschewed it as the sound could wake everyone up. There were times when I even avoided using the toilet at night because flushing was noisy.

Anju would keep dinner for me. I usually heated the plate of food in the microwave; at other times, I ate the food cold because turning on the microwave could be a loud affair at night. Anju and Arun had hectic schedules and little kids, and I didn't want to disturb them. I wasn't going to repay their kindness with inconsideration. Once in a while, Anju and Arun would be watching 'Law and Order' on TV when I got back, and Anju would serve me a hot dinner.

By the time I was finished with dinner, it would be nearly midnight. I would prepare the sofa bed and then study for two hours, after which I would sleep. Sometimes, Arun would walk into the room while I was studying and, in the loving tones of an elder brother, ask me to get some sleep. There was no doubt that the couple loved me deeply. They didn't charge any rent from me or have me pay for groceries or utilities. I was always a part of their weekend outings and they never intruded into my personal space. Arun always encouraged me and Anju always supported me.

❦

I had been staying at Arun and Anju's for nearly five months. I was earning now and it was time to look for accommodation of my own. Shared accommodation was my only choice as I didn't make enough to afford an independent place. In the first week of December, I saw an advertisement in the local newspaper. It was from someone who lived near my college and was looking for a flatmate. He turned out to be an Australian man of Croatian descent. When I called him up, he introduced himself as Anthony. Then he said, 'It will be $100 per week plus utilities on actual.' I took the offer in a jiffy.

Life was easier now that I was living a couple of blocks away from my college. Saving nearly two hours of commuting time every day, work was only a twenty-minute train ride away. It gave me more time to study, read and, sometimes, to rest and dream. With a room to myself, I also resumed my meditation.

Anthony and I didn't communicate much. Employed in the construction industry, he'd leave early in the morning and be back by mid-afternoon. I didn't know anything about the construction industry and he didn't know anything about computers. While I was a devout Hindu, he was a staunch Protestant. I was unfamiliar with Croatian culture and knew only a little about Australian culture while Anthony had simply no idea about India. We did have one thing in common though: we were both the 'quiet' type. And this was enough to strengthen our human bond because, through our silence, we accepted each other and respected each other's personal space. Unexpectedly, we became good friends when I helped him buy a second-hand computer.

One lazy weekend, two months after I'd moved in, he started talking about some person called Elvis Presley. Apparently, he was a rock star. Only, I had never heard of him.

'What? You've never heard of Elvis?' He didn't close his mouth after completing the question.

'No.'

'You are joking.'

'No.'

'Mate! You must be the first man on the planet who hasn't heard of Elvis.'

'Maybe!'

He threw his head back and cackled with laughter. Later that day, I happened to speak to my brother in India, and told him about this little incident.

'Ask him if he's heard of Lata Mangeshkar,' he said. 'Tell him she holds the Guinness world record for singing the most number of songs. Over 26,000!'

We both had a good laugh over the phone. No matter what, my brother Rajan supported me unconditionally.

For survival in Australia, however, I needed funds more than I needed laughter and comfort. At work, post-tax, I was making $254 per week. After the rent, utilities, train pass and groceries, I was left with roughly $50 but still partied once a week. Every Friday, I treated myself. In the morning, I bought a cappuccino, my favourite beverage. In the afternoon, I had orange juice; and, in the evening, I went to Hungry Jacks, a fast-food chain, for a Veggie Meal. It came with a delicious vegetarian burger, French fries and a soft drink.

There were three people at my party: I, me and myself. Never four, never two. There was no time, no thought of other friends, girlfriends or socializing. Every week, I also treated myself to a new book. I had realized that even if I could save $50 per week, it wouldn't suffice to pay for my college fees. Investing in books and building my knowledge base seemed a better option than building my bank balance.

Even though I never spoke about it, Greg could sense my concerns and the challenges that I was faced with. He once invited me to have lunch at his home with his wife and two boys. His wife, Linda, was a lovely lady and took the trouble to make lentils for me since she knew I was a vegetarian. Greg was kind to me and suggested I stay with them to save rent. I was touched at his generosity. Free accommodation would really help me save money. But I had always been a somewhat private person. I cherished my space in the quiet apartment I was in.

Besides, a free stay was not the long-term solution anyway. I had to be making more money. I continued to train and enhance my skills, and improve myself by constantly reading more books and learning new technologies. And I coded day and night. When I wasn't coding or studying, I meditated. You could wake me at midnight and ask me about the specs of a programming language. I would give you the correct answer. You could give me buggy software and I would look at it and point out precisely the error in it before even compiling and running it. It was almost like developing programming intuition. I couldn't afford a tutor, I had no mentor in programming and college teachers were too basic for my needs. I needed God to help me with my programming but he was busy restoring chaos in a twisted world. I had to rely on my own skills and, of course, books.

In my efforts to educate myself further, I decided to get Microsoft certification in systems engineering, and bought a set of books to study for this certification program. Manpower, a recruitment company, allowed candidates to come and take the online test on their premises. The day I went there, I met two wonderful people: Kieran Hawthorn and David Soo. Kieran was a Caucasian and looked every bit Australian, while David was of Chinese descent but born and raised in Australia.

After we chatted for a while, Kieran surprised me by saying he wanted to interview me for potential job opportunities with his clients. We sat down in one of the meeting rooms to talk.

'What other programming languages do you know?' he said.

Instead of answering his question, I said, 'Kieran, you'll leave Manpower real soon and start your own company.

'Excuse me?'

'Yes. And I'll be the first candidate you'll place with a client.'

He quickly closed the door, sat down beside me and murmured, 'How do you know? Are you psychic? I just started thinking about leaving last week.'

'When my intuition talks, I listen. I listen to my inner voice, Kieran, and it tells me what I just told you.'

'Will I do well in my business?'

'Yes. I have no doubt.'

Four weeks later, Kieran called me. From his own recruitment firm. He said there was an opportunity for a web programmer with Pure Commerce, a start-up based in the Australian Technology Park (ATP). The CEO was a twenty-six year-old called Daniel Lavecky. Kieran put me in touch with him.

Daniel ended up interviewing me three times in two weeks, and grilled me at every interview. During one of our conversations, I asked him how big the company was. Without giving me a direct answer, he told me that there were many stakeholders and contractors. After the interviews were done, I was told that someone would get back to me soon.

It was a Thursday and I was at work at TTA when my phone rang.

'Congratulations! You've got it,' Kieran said.

My heart skipped a beat.

'I have?'

'Yep. $40,000 package.'

Now we were talking. University seemed within reach.

'When do I start?'

'Daniel wants you to start asap. Monday.'

'But I have to give two weeks' notice.'

'I strongly recommend that you start on Monday because we don't want to lose this opportunity. I have already talked

about your visa situation and Daniel says he will have the
contract drawn out accordingly. I doubt we'll get a chance
like this again.'

It was true; I didn't want to lose this chance. Pure
Commerce specialized in building payment gateway
systems, one of the first companies in Australia to do multi-
currency payment processing online.

Right after this call, I broke the news to Greg and Joe,
telling them that I was leaving their company.

Greg took me in the meeting room, closing the door a
little harder than usual.

'Tell me now,' he said with a neutral expression. 'What's
the matter?'

'I want to leave TTA.'

'But I even offered you a free stay at my home!'

'I know, Greg. I'm sorry. I have to go because I need to
pay for my uni education.'

After some more discussion, where he tried to convince
me to stay on, we arrived at the subject of the notice period
rather abruptly.

'Well, you do some thinking and let us know on Monday.'

'Actually, I won't be coming to work on Monday.'

'What? You have to give us two weeks' notice.'

'I'm sorry, Greg, I can't because the new employer wants
me to start on Monday. Rest assured, my code is fully
documented.'

'This is insane.' His voice was a little raised now. I sensed
that he was more angry than sad.

'I'm sorry.'

'You think it over properly, mate,' Greg said tersely as we
finished the meeting.

This was April 1999 and I had worked at TTA for over
six months. I left that afternoon and didn't go back the

following Monday. The green bean that I was, I didn't value my relationship with Greg and Joe. What was even worse was that I knew this was not the way to quit, but was unable to resist the new job opportunity. I felt I couldn't afford to let it go as I needed the funds to pay for my education. Still, leaving as unprofessionally and ungratefully as I did was a mistake. A moral error. Professionally, I had done more than my fair share since I was only being paid for twenty hours whereas I had worked twice as many hours. Personally, I had thoroughly failed in repaying Greg's kindness. I owed both Greg and Joe an apology, something I never got around to doing.

I started at Pure Commerce with great enthusiasm. Other than me, there was just one more person working there: Daniel. I searched for other employees but there weren't any. I was his first and only employee and it would remain like that till the last day of my employment there. It didn't bother me though. I was being paid a good salary, the work was interesting, I had a personal phone on my desk and my computer had Internet access.

While I was working at Pure Commerce, I also managed to complete my two-year college diploma. In fast-track mode in a year's time. But this diploma was merely a milestone and not my destination. After finishing the course I had struggled so hard for, I realized that I had actually not learned much in the past year. My work experience had been far more rewarding. If I could, I would have dropped out of this course but that was not a possibility for it would mean a violation of my student visa and subsequent deportation from Australia. My heart was set on a university education and I wanted a proper degree, at least a bachelor's. At the same time, giving another three years to a bachelor's degree was not something I was prepared to do. I wanted to do it as fast as possible and get it out of the way so that I could focus on my career.

Meanwhile, there was a small issue with my diploma. I had scored well and was qualified to receive the diploma but it turned out that if I wanted to receive my certificate, I would have to pay the full fee for the second year too. This wasn't unreasonable but I just didn't have the $5,000 to pay for it. Not losing hope, I took my transcript and went to meet the course coordinator at the University of Western Sydney. He looked at my application and then examined my transcript, resume and the sample printouts of my software coding, all of which were neatly pinned to the application form.

'Why do you want to study at UWS?' he said.

'Because it's one of the best universities here, and offers just the course I want to do.'

'But you are already employed in the industry.'

'Yes, Mr Hosey, but I want to learn more about software modelling and business systems.'

He interviewed me for about fifteen minutes and subsequently marked on the application form: 'Exempted from the first year core subjects'.

'I've given you the maximum permissible exemption. Welcome to UWS,' he said.

Mr Hosey also approved my request to pay the tuition fees in instalments. My efforts at the business college weren't a waste after all. Not only did I save a year of my three-year degree, I also saved $14,000 in just tuition fees. I moved out of Anthony's place and into my own flat in a suburb called Parramatta as it was closer to the university. Suddenly, I felt there were no problems in my life. Everything had worked out.

During my daily commute on the train, I started writing articles for publications so I could better utilize my time.

These were largely technical journals and magazines based in the US. I was paid US $500 for every article. I stopped writing after a couple of months, however, due to the lack of time. You had to pitch the idea, write the article and supply sample code. None of this was hard, but it was time-consuming and time was something I didn't have to spare. I began using my commuting time to do my university assignments instead.

At Pure Commerce, pleased with my work and the revenue my applications were generating, Daniel gave me a $30,000 raise, spread over four months. While this was highly motivating, I was no longer excited about the company. There were two primary reasons for this. First, being the only employee here, there was no sharing of knowledge with teammates, no one to bounce ideas off. My spirit of competition was suffering because there was no one to compete against.

Secondly, I had already finished building the core software. It was the mango I had sucked dry and there was no juice in it now. Maintenance of systems was hardly a challenge for me. I wanted to build because building was the real deal. A software developer working on system maintenance is like an architect who, after erecting a world-class building, switches to the work of a janitor in the same building.

What next? I was itching to work on a larger and far more complex system, wanting to solve deeper and bigger problems. I rather enjoyed coding because it gave me an experience of complete absorption, almost like meditation. Just when I was contemplating moving from Pure Commerce, David Soo from Manpower contacted me. It was as if the Universe had been listening, and said, 'Granted.'

We met over a coffee and, as we chatted, he said, 'Someone like you should be working for a large corporate.'

'But who will hire me?' I asked.

'Why do you say that?'

I opened up to David and shared with him the work restrictions on my visa. Any public limited company would never take that chance, no matter how skilled I was. David, however, had a different view. He told me about an opportunity with a large company who would go the extra mile for me.

'But how will we resolve the visa issue?' I asked.

'Leave that to me.'

'There's another problem, David.'

Without waiting for him to respond, I told him that in the upcoming semester at university, there were two subjects that were only offered on a certain weekday, which meant taking a day off every week.

'Don't worry, we'll work this out.'

'Really?'

'Yep,' he said. 'Just don't mention any of this to the client in your interview. I'll handle it.'

Three days later, I was called for an interview with News Interactive, a division of News Corporation, the media giant. After a series of interviews, David struck a hard deal.

'I've some good news for you, Amit,' he said over the phone.

'Shoot!' I was so excited.

'Nah. Let's meet for dinner after work today.'

I went straight to Darling Harbour after work and we sat down at our usual table in Zafran, a plush Indian restaurant.

'Guess what,' David said in his usual matter-of-fact tone, 'I've got the package we were aiming for, along with visa sponsorship from News Corporation. Plus they'll give you a day off every week till you finish your degree *and* they'll pay for your uni.'

I was overwhelmed and my eyes became moist.

'And I kid you not, Amit,' David continued, 'this is only the beginning. Your technical competence is intimidating.'

I did not want to sit on my laurels but do better. I wanted to pledge my loyalty to David, I wanted to make him and my employer proud that they made the right decision in choosing me. But I was reluctant to take the sponsorship from News Corp because it came with the condition that I would have to work for them for a minimum period of four years. I had never liked getting tied down. I told David about this. 'I'll get the contract amended,' he said.

'For as long as you are in this business, David, and for as long as I'm in this industry,' I said, 'I give you my word, you will be my only agent.'

I held up my sparkling water while he raised his beer mug.

'Cheers, mate.'

Soon after joining News Corp, they appointed me a technical lead. I was going to lead an entire team of developers. Everything was bigger here: projects, teams, responsibilities and challenges as well as the rewards. The office itself was far grander than anything else I had encountered so far. Situated in a place called Pyrmont, the office was a waterfront property with floor-to-ceiling glass windows. There was even free coffee and a pool table. And no, this wasn't the distasteful instant coffee but the real thing. Two baristas made the most wonderful cafe lattes, cappuccinos and espressos. We were in the throes of the Internet boom and employers were trying everything to lure skilled IT professionals.

It was a highly productive environment at News, especially suited for geeks like me. I kept delivering on my projects and they kept assigning me more. David and I became really good friends. We met at least once a week, if not more. A black belt in tae kwon do, he was kind-hearted and competent. He was a relationship builder: while I always focused on performance and delivery, David made me see that interpersonal relationships at the workplace played an even more critical role than performance; technical excellence alone was not enough for professional growth.

While at News, a former Pure Commerce client contacted me. They ran a highly profitable online casino out of Antigua and the Barbuda Islands. They wanted to meet me and a meeting was scheduled with the founder and other executives at their head office in Antigua. The chairman, tall, slim and grey-haired, introduced himself as Otto. They offered me the role of technology director. It was a $750,000 package. This was not just a raise but a quantum leap from what I was making, far more than I could ever hope to make in Australia. In return, I had to build a payment gateway for them.

I was ready to take up the position except for a moral dilemma I found myself in. I wasn't sure I was OK working for a casino. The issue was resolved when I happened to meet a member of their customer service team while I was making a round of the office. He was replying to an email from an American customer who was begging for his transactions to be reversed because he had made a huge mistake. The American customer had gambled away $60,000 between his four credit cards. In his email, he wrote that he was going to lose his home. I asked the customer service person if anything could be done for this man. 'Don't worry, I get many emails like this on a daily basis,' he said, dismissing the man's plea.

I had to think no further. I told them I had to go back to Sydney to wrap up things there, and agreed to join them four weeks later. However, I had no intention of coming back. Till date, I don't know why I lied to them but it was a strange environment there. I felt suffocated and wanted to leave as soon as possible. People were losing their lifetime savings and homes, and I didn't want to be a part of it.

From Sydney, I spoke to the CEO and told him that my conscience didn't allow me to support a casino. News Corp, in the meanwhile, gave me a hefty pay rise of $25,000. They thought they had lost me.

⁕ᴥ⁕

Over dinner one night, David said, 'I think you're meant for a bigger role, Amit. They are underutilizing you at News.'

'You think so?'

'Yes, you should be heading an organization and not just projects.'

This was David's style. No matter how important the information, he always delivered it casually. There was no way of knowing if it was a spontaneous remark or if he had given it serious thought beforehand.

'Do you have something in mind?'

'You should meet, Greg,' he said.

'Who's Greg?'

'He makes technology blueprints for large organizations and needs someone like you.' That was all he said.

Two days later, he introduced me to Dr. Gregory Uppington. A PhD in enterprise integration and an IT veteran, Greg's humility was unearthly. Greg and I connected from the moment we first shook hands, and we went on to become close friends. He specialized in large-scale systems integration and was working as the chief information officer (CIO) for a start-up called Industry Wide Networks (IWN). He mentioned they were really struggling and desperately needed a sharp chief technology officer (CTO). Greg wanted me to take on that role.

I met with the CEO, Daniel Hilson or Dan as he was called. I loved his product and vision. They were using cutting-edge technologies and working on a data aggregation product way ahead of its time. After a series of interviews with Dan and his team, the company's board grilled me for three hours after offering me just a glass of water and before agreeing to my expectation of a quarter-million-dollar package.

The executive team at News Corp was not pleased to see my resignation. They tried to hold me back with more money and argued that I had numerous options at News. But what they didn't have for me was the enormous challenge that IWN's product had. Apart from the product they were working on, I was really attracted to Dan's vision and entrepreneurial traits. Here was a young CEO, in his early thirties, running his own show. I could learn much from him, I thought.

Within the first three days at IWN, I had studied their systems documentation, examined the software architecture and the systems design, glanced over the coding and identified the gaps. I came to a disturbing realization: the vision was great but the product wasn't as complicated or complex as they had made it out to be. There was no way it could absorb eight to ten hours of my time daily; an hour each day would do the job. I could not justify receiving such high salary.

I shared my findings with Dan and said, 'I don't think you need me full-time, Dan.'

'How you mean?'

'Well, I can guide the team and steer the product development by giving it just one hour daily. There's nothing for me for the remaining seven hours.'

He seemed intrigued by my statement and shook his head slightly. Perhaps he thought I was going to resign. A few moments passed in that uncomfortable silence.

'What do you suggest?' he asked finally.

'I can build a consulting division for you. Let me bring in revenues so I may pay for my own salary.'

He nodded in appreciation. A few days after our conversation, he scheduled a meeting with the world's biggest shopping mall company, Westfield. It was perfect timing. They were running a multimillion-dollar e-commerce project but were struggling with the delivery and integration. They gave us a seven-figure contract on the condition that I was going to be available to them full-time. I juggled between the two roles, leading the project at Westfield and handling the product team at IWN as their CTO. My employer continued to be IWN. I was pleased to generate revenue many times more than my salary.

This was 2000. I had landed in Australia in 1998 and had struggled to find a job that would pay me anything at all. Two years later, at twenty, I was sitting on an executive technology-management role with a more than decent salary package. Was this just due to my hard work? It would be foolish to think so. A transcendental element of grace was always there. Otherwise, there was no dearth of people who worked harder than I did and who were smarter than I was, but didn't find such success.

⁕⋇⋇⁕

In July that year, Rajan and my mother decided to visit me. They hadn't seen me in two years. I wanted to take my mother around, and thought of buying a car. One weekend, David and I stopped by the Saab showroom. We stood around for fifteen minutes, which felt like an eternity, hoping someone would come around to attend to us. Finally, a young man came over.

'Hi guys,' the salesman said. 'How can I help?'

When I asked for a test drive, he said there were no cars available.

I was taken aback at his indifferent attitude. Was he not interested in making a sale? I handed out my business card. His body language changed instantly. He said brightly, 'Should I see if there's a car for a test drive?'

'Tell you what,' I said, 'come and see me in my office, instead. Bring a demo car and the paperwork.'

'What time would suit you, Mr Sharma?' He shifted his gaze from the business card to me.

'11 a.m. Monday.'

'I'll be there.'

On Monday, when I was test-driving, he told me that he was the youngest in the dealership and the seniors had sent him to attend to us because they didn't think we were there to buy. It was raining lightly. I felt this was symbolic of Grace. Otherwise, how could someone who had winced at the thought of boarding a bus because the fare was $2 just two years ago now buy a convertible that was nearly $70,000? Grace.

I wanted to spend that money for my mother. I loved her in a way I loved no one else. It was not possible to ever repay her for the sacrifices she had made for me, the countless nights she had stayed awake with me when I was suffering from asthma and the way she had always stood by my side. It was not part of her job description to support my sadhana or my interest in astrology, chess, books and other things, but she had. I wanted her to have the best time in Sydney.

I did up my flat, buying new furniture, bed linen and toiletries. I stocked the fridge and the kitchen with all kinds of food items and bought gleaming new pots and pans for her. Finally, I drove to the airport to pick them up in my new car.

As soon as I saw my mother, I touched her feet, hugged her tight, kissed her cheeks. I hugged Rajan too. I was thrilled to see them.

'You've lost a lot of weight,' she said. 'You must be working hard at the cost of your health.'

'You've already started worrying!' I exclaimed.

'Now that I'm here for three months, I'll feed you well.'

'Tell me, Ma, do you like my new car?' I pressed a button and the roof folded into the trunk. 'I bought it for you.'

'May God bless you with much more,' she said. 'And may you always—'

'What about me, Amit?' Rajan interjected jokingly. 'I think I'll have better use of this car than our mother here.'

Ma was rather quiet in the car while Rajan was excited and chatty. I talked about the socio-economic system in Australia, the clean roads, my studies, my company and everything else I could think of. For every one of my statements, Rajan had ten questions.

Later that night, I asked my mother what was on her mind. She said, 'I know you had told me about your successes here over the phone but, after seeing it all with my own eyes, I don't have enough words to thank God. I'm feeling so content.'

In response, I just put my head at her feet. 'It's all because of your blessings, Ma.'

Her eyes filled with tears.

My mother loved her time in Australia and spent three months with me. It was one of the most memorable periods of my life because, for the first time, I was hosting my mother. And because she showered the love, care and blessings that only a mother could. She fed me a hearty breakfast every day and I came home to a delicious dinner at night. When I drove to work in the mornings, she would give me a pouch of freshly peeled almonds so I could eat them on the way while driving. As I left the house, she would come out with me to say bye. This was the first time in Australia that someone cared enough to see me off and wait at home for me when I returned. In the past two years, I had almost forgotten that I was not a machine but a human being. Her little caring gestures made me feel human again.

In those days, I was putting in long hours at work. There were times I came home only to sleep, but my mother never complained. I was unable to show her around the city in the way that I had wanted because I was always pressed for time, but she never made me feel guilty. 'I'm just happy to see you happy,' she would say.

One day, while I was sitting with her and talking about life in Australia, I said, 'Don't get me wrong, Ma. I love it here. This country has offered me so much but, to tell you the truth, my heart is not here.'

'Why, Amit, what's the matter?'

I opened up to her and told her how I missed putting those hours into my meditation, how I wanted to further my sadhana but just didn't have the time. I understood the role of education and I wasn't discounting the importance of money, but this was certainly not going to be the totality of my life. My goal had always been, and still remained, God.

'I wish to lead a more spiritual life one day,' I said.

'Whatever gives you happiness,' she said softly. 'I just know you'll never make a thoughtless move.'

I wasn't surprised at her acceptance of my statement. Nor did she encourage me to hanker after more money or status. She had always been ever supportive and understanding, as if she knew my innermost feelings.

While we were talking, Rajan walked into the room and said, 'You guys always scare me with your serious conversations!' I grinned at him. 'Ma, how come you always say yes to whatever Amit says?'

Ma just smiled but he was right. Beyond our temporary disagreements on minor issues, there had never been any conflict in my relationship with my mother. It could be because she never really opposed me or because she understood me completely, or both.

Rajan interrupted my flow of thoughts as he started mimicking a couple of Australians he had met that day. I had a hearty laugh because that was not how they spoke at all but, coming from Rajan, every word was comedic.

Before we knew it, it was time for our mother to go back to India. Rajan stayed back as he had been sponsored by a company and now had a work visa. After she left, I felt terrible because I had barely spent time with her. She had not come here to see my car and my flat, the buildings and the tourist attractions. She had come to see me.

⚜

In December, I finished my bachelor's degree, six months in advance. A three-year degree that was reduced to two years because of the exemptions eventually got completed in eighteen months because I did the additional subjects in summer and as well as winter school.

My life was finally stable now, with my basic education complete and a steady income coming in. Since I had arrived in Australia, I hadn't really had the time to focus on myself, on my inner life. My sadhana had not intensified or improved. Now, as things settled around me, the void that had always been within, but veiled briefly by my external pursuits, bared itself to me again.

My goal of renunciation was clear to me and I knew exactly where I was headed. But it wasn't time yet. I had to be certain I wasn't choosing the spiritual path as an escape from the material challenges of the world. To achieve the pinnacle of material success and *then* to walk away would be a far truer renunciation. If I had nothing to lose in the first place, what was I renouncing? I wanted to make sure my intent for spiritual life was clear and pure.

But I wondered if working for others was the way forward. No matter how much I made as an employee, I would have to work till I retired. And if I continued to work this way, when would I have the time to explore my own soul? Driving a convertible sports car to work didn't have the same charm now as it had in the first couple of months. My pay cheque, which had got me so excited earlier, felt like an ordinary piece of paper. The routine was starting to feel boring and I realized I needed to make some changes. It occurred to me that what I did for IWN, I could easily do for myself. I figured that building my own business would be an interesting and rewarding venture now.

IWN gave me a Christmas bonus of $20,000 after I earned more than two million dollars in revenue for them. I came home and showed Rajan the cheque.

'Wow! Let's celebrate,' he said.

'Absolutely. But first I have to send an important email.'

I wrote to Dan and then turned off my phone.

'Okay, let's go for a movie and a dinner. I really want to celebrate today.'

At the restaurant, I kept staring at the menu and chuckling to myself.

'What's the matter, why are you laughing?'

'You know, brother, life's like a menu. We have to make choices, we can't have everything. Even if we can afford it all, even if we want to eat it all, we simply can't. We must pick what delights us and not just order the first item on the menu. Today, I've made a choice too.'

'I get nervous with your cryptic talks, man. What did you do? What choice? Tell me in plain words.'

'I quit.'

'Can I get you some drinks to start with, gentlemen?' the waiter intervened.

'In a few minutes, please.' Rajan sent him away, staring at me in shock.

'You what? You quit? I thought you got a bonus cheque, not severance payment.'

The tension on his face made me want to laugh. 'It was a bonus cheque. But I emailed my resignation after I came home.'

'But *why?*'

'Because when I was driving back home today, I had a realization.'

'What realization? Oh please, say it clearly. What are you up to?'

'Why don't we order something first?'

'No. We are not ordering anything till you tell me why you quit. And what's this realization business?'

'Well, so far, I've been ordering the first item on the menu. My logic was to achieve what I didn't have so that I could be happy. When I was unemployed, I wanted to be a programmer. When I became a programmer, I aimed to be a software architect. Then I became a technical lead, a technical manager, a technical director and finally a CTO. I guess this policy has served me till now. But I'd be a dunce to continue like this. Am I happy? Is this what I want to do? No, brother, no. This is not what I want to do and this is not what I was born to do.

'In the board meeting today, one of the members was sixty-five years old and still worried about getting a parking ticket. As he crunched numbers, he was coughing and sick but forced himself to attend the meeting. Why do we earn and why do we learn? What is growth? What is progress?'

'Can I get you something now, gentlemen?'

'A salad, a bruschetta, a coke and a sparkling water with a slice of lemon,' I said. 'Two vegetarian pennes for the main and one of them with bocconcini cheese, please.'

'Did you want anything else?' I asked Rajan. He shook his head.

'I don't want to be like that old board member,' I continued. 'A dog never becomes the master. I don't wish to be an employee anymore. I want to be my own boss, the captain of my ship.'

'But what will you do?'

'I'll start my own business.'

'What about capital? You need an office and a team. How will it all happen?'

'I don't have the answers yet, but I've decided I'll work for ten more years. I'll retire at thirty, no matter what. The only way I can do that is to build my own business.'

'But what if the business doesn't do well? We have no background in business.'

'It doesn't matter. I've decided on a course and nothing can stop me.'

'But what if God has other plans for you? I haven't seen anyone retiring at thirty.'

I laughed. 'This may be God's menu but I'm the customer here. I'll decide what I want to eat.'

'But what will you do after retiring?'

'I plan to meet the Creator. I would like to see who designed the menu for me.'

'And what does *that* mean?'

'It means what I just said. I'd like to meet God.'

'What God? What *are* you talking about? Stop torturing me, Amit. Just say it clearly please.'

'I want to devote my life to my search for Truth.'

'Your whole life?'

'Whatever it takes.'

'What if you change your mind tomorrow?'

'Of course I'll change my mind. The mind is always changing. It's the nature of the beast. What won't change, however, is my resolution. I solemnly declare that I'll retire at thirty, exactly ten years from now.'

'What's the big deal about being thirty?'

'By then, I know I'll have earned the money I need. And I'll be ready to move on. Besides, if I can't build a business in ten years, that means I'm not fit for business. Ten years is long enough to succeed at something.'

Rajan sat in stunned silence. I nudged him to eat and consoled him as well, saying there were still ten years to go and that I would always be by his side. The food was served and, for the first time in years, I was no longer in a rush. The soft but crunchy bread, the succulent balls of fresh mozzarella in my penne, the taste of fresh greens, the tickle of black pepper, the flavour of dill—I experienced them all. They came, one by one, and mingled on my tongue in a strange blend of bliss and awareness. And I savoured every bite. I wasn't just eating my food; I certainly wasn't gulping it down. I was experiencing it.

Sip by sip, I enjoyed the sparkling water, its bubbles reminding me of the rush of desires in the human mind. They would continue to rise till the water turned flat, but this did not mean I had to drink hurriedly. Bubbles of ambition and desire, of situation and circumstance, of thought and emotion, would keep emerging, but I still had the option of enjoying my drink one sip at a time, at my own pace. These bubbles were good, they were even necessary. They were not to be loathed but enjoyed, for they had made the flat water sparkle in the first place.

SIX

Porsche and More

It was time to start my own IT consulting business. I could not afford an office or a team, so I started out in my own apartment, with barely any capital. I was certain of making it big but my plans got a jolt when I ran from pillar to post and failed to get a contract from my existing contacts. This was because the Internet bubble had just burst, the financial markets were in the doldrums, consumer sentiment was weak and corporate spending was at an all-time low.

To make matters worse, I realized that I had practically no knowledge of starting or building a business. I had mistakenly thought that my technical competence was sufficient to generate business. Well, it wasn't. To make up for my lack of skills and learn some formal tricks of the trade, I enrolled for an MBA program at the University of Technology Sydney.

Four months later, I saw a contract opportunity with Eclipse Group, a web design enterprise and a fully-owned subsidiary of Deloitte Consulting, one of the world's top five consulting firms. A meeting with their CEO, Michael Kean, was arranged. At the meeting, I learnt that Eclipse Group wanted to generate more revenue from software rather than from web design. This was because there was more money in software. Software was my area of specialization, of course, and I didn't think this was a coincidence. They signed me up at $1,000 per day to grow and lead the software development practice.

I accompanied Mike to most executive meetings and presentations. The reason customers liked me, they said, was because I fearlessly spoke my mind. I didn't follow the usual method, where consultants simply endorsed the decisions the client had already made. My role was instrumental in securing more business from General Motors and Dairy Farmers. Both were multibillion-dollar organizations, the former being much bigger. When I assessed the technology blueprint of the two companies, I told the CIOs at both organizations that they were wasting money by buying a particular software, a content management solution.

A few months later, Mike invited me for a coffee at the Crowne Plaza in Melbourne. Coming to the point quickly, he said wanted me to think about taking on a bigger role—something more permanent at Deloitte. He went on to say that he was retiring and looking for a successor to head Eclipse Group. Clearly, he was hinting at a career for me at Deloitte but I didn't want employment. I was still quiet when he said, 'You know what our biggest challenge is?'

I said, 'In terms of clients?'

'No. In terms of you.'

I smiled.

'You see, our biggest challenge is to find a challenge for you.'

I was deeply impressed at his reading. It was true. Whenever something stopped challenging me, I would just move on.

'And do you know what the biggest challenge for you is?'

'To stay motivated?'

'Maybe. But the real challenge for you will be to pick the right option. Life is going to present you with many choices and, obviously, your future will depend on your choices.'

His profound statement, laced with wisdom, has stayed with me.

Meanwhile, my consulting practice grew. I hired a small team and invested every single cent of my profits in the development of an enterprise search engine; it was like Google but meant only for companies.

Over the next two years, I got my Australian permanent residency, finished my MBA, set up a software development centre in India and travelled to New York to start a branch office. The New York operation, however, didn't do as well as I had expected, and Sydney needed my attention, so I curtailed my ambition and focused more on my Australian operations.

Revenues from the Australian business flowed in, and I was keen to invest them in areas other than just product development. A year later, in 2003, I decided to start an office in Silicon Valley. I needed an infusion of institutional capital to take my product to the broader market segment. I also needed someone to manage my Australian operations.

I had met Andi at a client's and we had become friends. We often played chess together. I hired him to work for me. He wanted to build his own company, so we agreed that while looking after my business, Andi could also work on his own product, unrelated to our offerings, so that there was no conflict of interest. After all, that's how Deloitte had supported me.

I shifted to California temporarily, leaving the reins of the Australian operations in Andi's hands. After staying in a serviced apartment for a few weeks, I moved in with Ashwani Verma, a distant cousin, and his wife Monika. They opened the doors of their home, as well as their hearts, for me. A great support, they helped me take my mind off work.

I spent a few months in California pitching my company to various venture capitalists. Back in Australia, however, we didn't close any major deals in my absence. With mounting expenses in India and California, I unexpectedly found myself in the middle of a severe cash crunch. Finally, DFJ, a tier-one venture capital firm in Silicon Valley, showed interest in investing. After I presented to all the partners in the firm, I was certain that the funding of seven million dollars was on its way.

A couple of days after the presentation, my phone rang. It was Josh Stein, my contact at DFJ. My mouth went dry. I knew he was going to talk about the terms sheet. God had materialized the money for me. Josh spoke for a couple of minutes but I couldn't register anything he said; I was just waiting to hear the good news. Finally, his words came through. 'Unfortunately, other partners are not keen at this time, but I think you have a great product and you should pursue other investors.' He said some other things that I don't remember.

I was shattered. I had no other real tangible leads. I called Keith for consolation. Keith Taylor, in his late forties, was a good friend and the chief financial officer (CFO) of a start-up in Silicon Valley. I had met him through an online reference soon after arriving in the US. He had helped me with the financial model for raising equity along with the venture capital pitches. Soon, we were meeting every Sunday morning for a coffee and a sandwich. He told me not to worry and that I would find some other leads. But I was completely lost.

I spoke to Ashwani and he suggested I take a break. I had been working day and night across three time zones for the last several months. I also called Arun, who had moved from Sydney to Toronto two years ago. He asked me to visit him for a few days. I boarded the next flight to Toronto.

The city was a good change for me. We went out Friday evening and the entire day on Saturday. On Saturday night, I checked my email to find one from Andi. It was his resignation letter, stating he would not be coming to work Monday onwards. Monday? He was supposed to give me a month's notice. I called Andi but got his voicemail instead. I left messages but did not receive his call. How could he not honour the notice period?

Then it hit me that he had left me exactly the way I had left TTA back in 1998. It was payback time. I immediately thought about my clients and my employees. How would I support them? I had to go to Sydney right away. There were no direct flights available, so I hopped through four connections to reach Sydney.

This was now October 2004; I had been away for seven months. Upon reaching Sydney, I found out that the situation was much worse than I had thought. Andi's resignation was only the last nail in the coffin; much had already happened in my absence. In a direct conflict of interest, Andi had offered my customers the same services through his company. Rumour spread that my company had gone belly up. My major customers jumped ship in panic, thinking they would not get technical support from us any longer. A couple of other customers contracted with Andi's company directly, and all prospective customers shied away.

This storm had been quietly raging in Australia while I had been focusing on raising equity capital in the US, totally unaware of what was going on. I tried to salvage the situation and met with my customers, but it was very hard to win them back. Being unavailable for seven months was equal to seventy years in the Internet age; my clients had lost confidence in me.

One customer, a dairy company called Bega Cheese, stood by me and asked me to continue the work. They were a small client but I was happy that I had an active client reference. I also knew that sooner or later, I would sign up new projects, but I needed money right away to keep the India office going. This office formed my technical team and I couldn't do without them. So, I decided to sell my assets, including my house.

I had been looking for a change of scene in any case, and figured this was a good time to move; Canada was my next destination. I wanted to build a business in a bigger economy. By that time, Rajan had been married for over a year to a wonderful person called Pooja. I called her PB, short for Pooja Bhabhi. PB was like a mother to me and took care of me at every step. Together, Rajan and PB were my backbone. The three of us had lived together in Australia. When I told them I was moving to Canada, they announced they would come with me.

'You don't have to move because of me,' I protested, 'everything is going so well for you here.'

'No, Amit. We will live wherever you live. We'll live together,' said PB warmly.

'Don't worry about me. I'm fine. Seriously. There's no guarantee I'll even stay in Canada. Most likely, I'll move to the US.'

'That's fine, we'll still be closer to you.'

'But why do you want to quit your jobs and take this major step?'

'You know, even though I look up to you, you are still my younger brother,' said Rajan. 'I can't stop feeling protective about you, I'm concerned about you. I know you can rebuild your business and I want to support you. I'll take care of all the living expenses.'

'Are you both sure you want to move to Canada?'

'Yes,' they chorused. 'We are where you are. Nothing else matters.'

I laughed heartily. 'Alright then, tighten your seat belts, kids. We're gonna have one helluva time in Canada.'

Then PB asked, 'Tell me honestly, you are stressed, aren't you?'

'You want to know the truth? Will you believe me?'

'Of course.'

'Then listen carefully. The truth is that I'm greatly relieved. I had stopped stressing on my return flight to Sydney, and I can't be bothered by what is past. I'm happy because I'm free again and I'm ready to build again. I've always enjoyed building more than running. I know exactly what I need to do now. In fact, I've already thought about the car I'm going to buy next year.'

'Oh really!' PB was always excited about everything I said or did. My brother shook his head disbelievingly.

'Tell us, tell us, which car will you buy next year?'

I turned my laptop towards them.

'Oh my God! A Porsche!' PB clapped in excitement.

'Yes, I was already selecting the model.'

'I know you'll do it,' said PB.

'Can we come back to earth, Amit, if you don't mind?' Rajan said. 'We've just sold our house and everything else of any monetary value. We're in a grave situation here. Don't you think we should be a little practical?'

I laughed again. 'Watch me, brother, wait till you see me in action. Before the end of next year, I promise I'll have this seal-grey baby. Not financed, rented or leased, but a fully owned car.

'I know he'll do it,' PB exclaimed.

'You guys are unbelievable,' Rajan muttered in exasperation.

'Well, we'll revisit this topic next year and then you tell me,' I said.

'Oh, the lion's injured but hasn't forgot to hunt,' Rajan said.

'Porsche, bro, Porsche. Next year. A Porsche parked in our own house.

Alright, I want to celebrate this promise. I want to celebrate our car and new house in advance. Put that black dress on, PB. We're going for the finest Italian cuisine in town.'

⁕⋇⋇⁕

Rajan and PB moved to Canada first. I had to stay back for at least six weeks to wrap things up. I started hunting for a small, short-term contract to better utilize my time. Six weeks was too brief a period but I wasn't prepared to waste even a moment. I had to get back on my feet and earn my livelihood again. This was another opportunity that destiny was throwing my way and I could have easily renounced the world now; in fact, I was tempted to. Yet, a part of me knew clearly that to do so at this time would be escapism. It would also be an untrue renunciation because, almost penniless, what did I have to renounce anyway? I also wanted to build from scratch to prove to myself that the first time round wasn't a fluke. I wanted to be sure that I did indeed have the competence and conviction to script my own destiny.

A few days later, New South Wales Police (NSWP) offered me a senior role, asking me to lead the software architecture team working on a police investigations system. It was a three-month contract with an extension of equal duration, which meant I would have to stay back for six months.

Staying the additional months also fulfilled the criteria for acquiring my Australian citizenship, something I looked forward to. I felt a certain loyalty towards Australia because this country had extended to me every opportunity to further myself, to spread my wings and fly high. It had given me quality education and just the right social and professional environment.

This was also a good opportunity to rebuild my business, sign on new customers and regain my confidence. I took up the role NSWP was offering me. Going through my Rolodex, I called everyone I knew, and out of those calls came opportunities worth many thousands of dollars. I signed on other customers.

In July 2005, a mere seven months later, I moved to Canada as a millionaire. A week later, a seal-grey top-model Porsche, a Carerra 4S, was parked in the garage of our four-bedroom house in Canada. I launched a marketing campaign to develop my business, and signed up seven new customers within a span of five weeks. An associate company now looked after my customers in Australia. I built a customer base in India and also signed on small customers in the US. Cash was flowing, profits were good and I was back in business.

I was ready to take a break now and there was no better way than to take the Porsche for a spin. I decided to go on a four-week circuit ranging the East Coast. I turned my phone off and just drove, stopping wherever I felt like. From golf resorts in Ontario to spa resorts in the eastern townships of Quebec, from there to Boston and back, I explored many places. These were not the highlights of the trip though. On my way to New York, I got a speeding ticket and promised myself I would behave for the rest of the trip. This was a promise I broke promptly, but I ended up having an experience of a lifetime, creating a memory I would never forget.

It happened on a highway in Vermont. No, I didn't meet with an accident but I think I lost my sanity for a minute when I chose to step on the gas and reach a speed of 280 km per hour. My eyes were locked on the road ahead and there was no time to see the scenery that went past in a blur. I remember thinking of Einstein after I slowed down to the legal speed limit. Time was truly relative. At 280 km per hour, even though I was at that speed for no more than thirty seconds, I felt I had lived through a lifetime. At the core of the thrill was a sense of deep fear. A lapse in concentration for even a couple of seconds could have resulted in complete disaster. But the anticipation of the thrill had completely overridden my reason. I remember feeling compelled to step on the gas.

Interestingly, at that fast and illegal speed, I ended up having an eternal and legitimate experience—the experience of unusual stillness and remarkable awareness. That is why every second felt so much longer to me, and those moments were filled with the most intense quietude. The faster I'd gone, the quieter it had become.

Two weeks later, I turned on the phone to inform my brother that I was well, and found I had quite a few voicemails. One of them was a message about my sister, who was admitted to a hospital because she had been having seizures and convulsions. She had been asking for me. I felt terrible. Here I was, having turned off my phone so I could have fun and be undisturbed, only to discover my sister had really needed me and I had not been available.

I first spoke to mother and then called Didi. She was still in the hospital. The MRI had revealed a tumour in her brain. I cut short my vacation, put everything on hold and took the next flight to India. I rushed to the hospital in Patiala as soon as I landed in New Delhi.

She hugged me tight and cried. 'I've missed you so much. I've thought about you every moment. I was dying to hear your voice, just once.'

'I'm sorry, Didi, I'd turned off my phone for a few days.'

'Will I be okay?'

'Just okay? I promise you'll feel even better than before.'

'I'm worried about Daksh, he's only eight. He needs me.' She began sobbing.

'Why are you talking like this, Didi? I promise you everything will be just fine. Nothing will happen to you. What am I here for?'

I kissed her head, I kissed her forehead, I kissed her cheeks, I hugged her tight till she calmed down. I promised her I would not leave India till she had completely recovered.

Her husband, Suvi, and I took her to Delhi. The chief neurosurgeon recommended immediate surgery. 'There's a 1 per cent chance of loss of life, 2 per cent chance of loss of memory and 13 per cent chance of loss of vision,' the surgeon said. 'You need to sign here to indicate you understand and accept this.'

The surgeon's look had conviction but no assurance or emotion; my brother-in-law's eyes held fear and anxiety. For the first time in my life, I had a sinking feeling in my stomach. I had been helpless before, but this was different. If anything went wrong now, there was no road to recovery, no way of making things alright. I had no control over this situation and no medical insights either. But I had one thing, which gave me the courage to put my hand on Suvi's shoulder to steady him as he signed. Faith. I had faith. For I knew it was not her time yet.

I remember feeling weak as she hugged me before being taken to the operation theatre. A tear rolled down from the corner of her eye as she waved at me quietly. Later, in the ICU, looking at her shaved head, her eyes huge in her round, pale face, she had looked like a beautiful Buddhist nun. I cannot forget how, when she was brought back to the hospital room, she had smiled like a child at the sight of a room full of flowers. But the memory that stays with me is the one where she is back home, healthy and happy, her laughter filling the house, her joie de vivre intact.

Three months later, I went back to Canada and resumed the Canadian operations, signing on many new customers. After that, I shifted to Silicon Valley once more to revive my old contacts, secure new customers and, above all, shop for investors for my new business. In my spare time, I drove around the Valley; it was a lovely time of year to be there. I had the chance to meet wonderful people, and had many an inspiring conversation with brilliant minds. Keith and I continued to meet on Sundays.

One day, I happened to get an email from a person called Atul Sharma. Professionally, I had known Atul from my New York days when he was a vice-president with Lehman Brothers. At this time, he was a senior executive with Barclays Bank in London. Atul wrote about his upcoming plan that involved large-scale banking projects with leading web technologies. On top of his agenda was innovation engineering: he wanted to roll out software that enabled better internal and external communication among the various stakeholders. We gave him an online demo of my search product and he immediately saw the potential.

The product could take data warehousing and business intelligence to an entirely new level.

Atul asked me to establish a presence in London. He was a sharp and incredibly driven individual; clients like him were vital for a start-up like mine. Being in London also meant I could explore the European market since I already had small customers in Denmark, Norway and Holland. In December 2006, I moved to London. Barclays turned out to be a major customer but this relationship was short-lived, the result of a sudden management change at Barclays coupled with the financial market crisis. This was June 2007.

Now, I finally paused and took a long look at myself. I still had to discover the truth of my existence. My desire to meet God was waiting to be fulfilled. This life I was living at the moment was good, was even true, but this was not the only truth and certainly not the eternal truth I longed for. It was time to move back to India. It was time to find my God.

I sold my Porsche and gave the proceeds to some ISKCON devotees I knew in Australia. I had enjoyed it just as I had enjoyed all my other possessions. I will not deny that I had made the most of my wealth and luxurious lifestyle. It was a delight to stay at the suite in the W Hotel in New York or at the Royal Mirage in Dubai, have high tea at the Ritz Carlton in London and savour vegetarian meals in San Francisco, pastas in Venice and desserts in Paris.

Travelling in business class was a pleasure as was visiting the stunning locales in Switzerland, rejuvenating spa resorts in California, beaches in Australia and mountains in New Zealand. I liked having a cook and a cleaner and someone to launder my designer clothes. I wore shirts made from ultra-fine cotton with my customized business suits; expensive and elegant watches in graphite metal and sapphire glass completed my ensemble. My wardrobe had the latest outfits from Versace, Armani, Prada, Bvlgari, Tag Heur, Longines, Mont Blanc...

Yet, wealth had never been my primary focus. Whether big or small, a goal once attained turns into a mere experience and then just a memory. My luxurious lifestyle had been a stepping stone in my journey. I knew very well that material success did not make me who I was, it did not define me in any way. And I was ready to give it all up now.

The Universe, however, didn't seem ready just yet. From London, I went for a short vacation to Canada before moving back to India. There, I met a man called Vivek Dhume, an acquaintance of Rajan's. I liked him instantly.

'It's my dream to do something in India,' he said at our first meeting.

I said, 'Well, I'm going to India permanently.'

'Will you be doing some business there?'

'Not really. I just want to take a break. I may do some stock trading to keep me busy.'

'Well, won't it be nice if we did something for India?' he said.

'Yes, but I have a different goal.'

'Can you share it with me?'

'How about over a bite tomorrow?'

We met the following day in a quiet restaurant called Zen Garden, where they served great vegetarian food.

'You see, Vivek, I'm financially taken care of and don't have the pressure of working to sustain myself. I've seen whatever I wanted to see in terms of material comforts and have no more desires on that front. Now, I want to devote my life to self-discovery and realization. I'm going to renounce and become an ascetic.'

Vivek stopped eating. We were the only customers in the restaurant. Complete silence ensued.

'You mean, you'll renounce as in renounce, like become a sadhu?'

'Yes.'

After a long pause, he asked, 'When will you do this?'

I'm glad he didn't ask me why I was going to renounce. There was no answer to that question.

'I can't disclose the date but I can tell you it'll be within the next three years.'

'You mean you'll actually leave everything and put on a robe?'

'Yes.'

'But what about the next three years?'

'I'm going to India to spend some time with my parents.'

'So, you won't work at all?'

'I'll be twenty-eight soon and am open to working till I'm thirty. In fact, I'm sitting on substantial savings and I don't mind investing the money in a new venture since I plan to give it up anyway. It's better to use it for creating employment for others than just leaving it the way it is.'

'But why did you earn it in the first place if you knew you would leave it all one day?'

'I never focused on earning it, Vivek. I was simply doing my karma, growing my business, and I was enjoying it. Money was not my goal, it was merely the consequence of intelligent decisions. Now, I wish to go in solitude and do intense sadhana.'

'Will you never come back from your sadhana?'

'I will. I just don't know when. It depends on how long it takes me to attain that transcendental state.'

'After you come back, won't you need a place to stay?'

'Yes, I will.'

'And you will have living expenses once you come back, right?'

'That's right.'

'So, why don't we build something in India? We can invest equally. You can renounce as per your plan but let the business pay you a stipend every month once you come back,' he proposed. 'We'll make a little place for you in the mountains.'

The idea sounded good. This way, I could always remain independent. I asked, 'Who will run the business? I can set it up and make it profitable but I won't be there to run it.'

'I'll run it.'

'You mean, you'll move to India?'

'Yes.'

'With your family?'

'Yes.'

'Are you sure?'

'Positive.'

I ate my tofu thoughtfully while Vivek watched me. Neither of us spoke for a while.

I said, 'You do know that I will go away, Vivek, and I will only return once I attain my goal.'

'I believe you.'

'So long as we are clear,' I said. 'I'll leave as soon as the business is profitable.'

'Fine.'

'I'll renounce my wealth to you, for you. A little gift.'

He was speechless. When he finally found his voice, he said, 'Why me, Amit? Why not leave it for your family?'

'I guess you'll find out one day.'

'No, I can't take so much from you.'

'I've already decided this, Vivek.'

'Anyway, we'll see to it later.'

'No, I'm serious. I want to renounce properly. We have to settle it now. Please don't expect me to be a part of the business once I walk away.'

He was quiet again. I knew this was neither my plan nor Vivek's; it was the Universe's way of doing things. What else could explain two people meeting for the first time and not only sharing their financials but pledging their entire corpus of savings? We had started our discussion over our entrées and everything was finalized before we ordered dessert.

SEVEN

The Renunciation

The following day, Vivek and I met to work out the details of our business. We had decided we would do something together but neither of us actually knew what we were going to do. He suggested growing my software business but I was bored with software. I had done it for nearly ten years now.

The cafe where we were sitting was full of customers and rather noisy. We decided to take a stroll and find a quiet place. Just a few shops down was a juice bar; it had no customers. We sat down and ordered a couple of smoothies.

Looking around, Vivek said suddenly, 'You know, there are no juice bars like this in India.'

'There are, but only in the big cities, I reckon.'

'But I haven't seen any chain of juice bars.'

'There are numerous roadside carts offering juices.'

'Yes, but what about a premium offering for those who care about health and hygiene?'

'You know what, it doesn't sound like a bad idea actually.'

We brainstormed for an hour and, without any further market research, decided that we would start a chain of juice bars in India. I wasn't sure if it was our casual attitude towards money or faith in each other that allowed us to simply put our chips on a business we had no knowledge of whatsoever. We agreed that I would start this enterprise in India and build the team, while Vivek would join me two years later.

⁂

In September 2007, I moved back to India. My parents were living in the same old house. My father was still driving his old scooter. The TV, sound system, furniture … everything looked old and shabby. All these years, I had travelled to India but had completely failed to notice how my parents were living. A deep sense of guilt washed over me. Even with all my wealth, I had been of no use to my parents.

I couldn't make up for the past but I could build for the present. I bought them a new house, furniture, gadgets and everything else I thought they might like. I bought them two new cars and hired a full-time driver as well; I didn't want them to use the scooter any longer.

But with all this came a realization: objects don't make up for what objects can't make up for. My father, a simple man, cared little about gadgets and cars. Both he and my mother were used to leading a certain life; after all, they had always lived that way. My arrangements had come a little too late. My father continued to use his old scooter most of the time.

When I asked him about this, he said simply, 'You're back to live in India. What more can we ask for?'

Repeatedly, Ma expressed how happy she was to have me back and to be able to feed me again. Seeing their happiness, I could not muster up the courage to share with them the fact that this joy was short-lived and that I was going to leave in the foreseeable future. I only shared my business plans with them. Even though my mother had never opposed me and my father always supported me, I couldn't figure out how to start this conversation. Besides, I was getting increasingly busy with building the new business, and didn't manage to find an appropriate moment to broach the topic.

Meanwhile, my software business was still obliged to fulfil its current and active contracts with customers in Canada, Australia, Holland and the US. I wanted to focus on the new business as, this time, it was not just about my savings but Vivek's as well. I wanted to do a thorough job and come through. So, I began wrapping up my software business in North America, Australia and India which, due to the nature of customer contracts, was an eighteen-month process.

Meanwhile, Vivek and I also acquired an Ayurvedic health-care company. Engaging a team of top doctors in the industry, we came up with a product range of seven unique health boosters. The company broke even within the first eighteen months.

Vivek moved back with his family in the third quarter of 2009. The company was turning around fast. By the end of that year, the company was in profit; in fact, we had several current orders and many more worth millions of dollars in the pipeline. I gently reminded Vivek that I would leave soon.

Another couple of months later, we saw a block of land in the mountains. Vivek and I stood on that land and thought it was a good place to be in after I returned from my sadhana. I told him that my only requirement was a meditation hall, around ten small rooms, a kitchen and a small cottage. But he gave me a bigger vision.

'We'll have nice pathways here, with fragrant creepers growing along both sides; there can also be trees arching over the paths. We'll have trees as wind-breaker around the periphery of the property and a pond in the middle. I'll get a special type of feed which, once placed in pots hung from the trees, will attract all sorts of coloured birds. We'll also have special meditation huts with thatched roofs. And it would be lovely to have deer running around. This place is going to be a heaven on earth.'

We finalized the deal for the land. On the way back from the mountains, Vivek and I discussed the monthly stipend the company would pay me, and settled on Rs 10,000. This was just a fraction, less than 2 per cent of what I would have earned had I invested my capital in a low-interest secure financial instrument like a term deposit. But it was enough for my needs.

I made a trip to Australia and Canada in late 2009 to meet my friends and family. My mother was in Canada visiting Rajan at the time. I wanted to see everyone once before marking my departure from the material world. I didn't know when they would be able to see me again. One evening, I was alone with my mother. 'You know, Ma, soon I'll leave for sadhana?' She turned pale.

'You already do sadhana, you sit in meditative absorption all the time, you have everything, my son. Why do you still want to go away?'

'You are right, Ma. But, God forbid, should something untoward happen to you or my other loved ones, the pain I experience will be far deeper than any sentiment I may feel at losing someone I don't care about or don't know. This means I'm still attached, still biased. I want to feel the same pain and the same love for all beings. To become impartial or, putting it another way, to have unconditional love for all, I need to be in solitude for a while. Plus, the vision of God I had earlier was dreamlike, Ma. I want something more concrete, more real.'

'As always, I don't have any response to your statements. All I have is this faith in you that you'll only take the right step, whatever it may be.'

I put my head in her lap. I knew this was the last time I would have this opportunity to experience my mother's love; it would not be possible after renunciation. In her incredible acceptance of my decision, I also saw deep pain. But my resolve did not break. I did what I had to because this was the only way I saw to quench the thirst of my soul. Maybe Prof. Sharma was right after all: I was all head and no heart.

I came back to India. In my drafts folder quietly sat the painful departure notes I had written for my loved ones while in Canada. Each note basically said that I was sorry for leaving them in this way but I had to take this step. I had long wanted to do this, and it was all I wanted from my life.

I got power of attorneys drafted for my personal as well as company assets. I left Vivek with exclusive control and transferred my assets in his name. The lawyer advised me against this but his job, I told him, was to execute and not advise. I could have given my wealth to my beloved family but I felt that this wouldn't be true renunciation.

On 15 March 2010, I gave my father a tight hug before leaving the house. I had breakfast at my sister's place and said goodbye to her. At work, I had a normal day. I printed letters and sealed envelopes. I made handover notes. I wrote cheques for some people out of the funds still sitting in my account—I wanted to give away every last penny I had and only live off the stipend money. Some investments were in a lock-in period so I couldn't liquidate them. Meanwhile, I had informed my bankers a couple of months ago of my decision, and made sure there were no debts to be cleared. My parents were financially secure as they both received pensions. My siblings were also comfortably off. My employees would be looked after by Vivek.

I had a nice lunch with Manik, a senior manager in our company, and a good friend. I told him I wanted to enjoy that day, and we went for a coffee. Vivek was out of town for a customer meeting. In the evening, I called Sandeep, my driver, who brought the car around.

'Railway station,' I said.

Sandeep was an extremely trustworthy person and quite attached to me. We had had many moments of laughter in the past thirty months. As he drove, we were both silent. I wasn't thinking about the present or the future; I wasn't thinking at all. I was simply quiet, the way I had been when I was leaving for Australia. These moments, when you are aware but not thinking, are blessed.

After a while, I let the thoughts enter. I reflected on the people I was about to leave and people I had already left behind. I had had my share of relationships, both platonic and intimate. Until I was about twenty-five, I had absolutely no time for anything other than my immediate priorities — work and meditation. Gradually, it had dawned on me that I had missed something very important: I had not experienced myself completely. I had studied about purusha and prakriti, Shiva and Shakti, yin and yang; I had studied tantra and done tantric practices. But my understanding of sexual union in tantra was superficial; I had no practical experience.

Always influenced by religious principles, I used to think that celibacy was essential for self-realization, a view I later found to be baseless and erroneous. I had known many girls and some had wanted me, but I had been driven by my own beliefs and wasn't ready for intimacy. It was also true that I didn't really feel the need for relationships. I had tried to reciprocate, I had cared about certain people, loved them even, but I couldn't feel any attachment to them; their presence or absence didn't make any difference to my state of mind.

'The trouble is,' one girl had said, 'there's nothing I can offer you because you have no needs.'

She wasn't entirely wrong. My heart was always in the Himalayas. I longed to experience the state the Buddha had realized, the state yogic scriptures talked about, the transcendence the Vedas preached, the samadhi the ancient sages talked of. My samskaras, innate tendencies, continuously pulled me towards that state of being. The more wealth I created, the stronger this urge got, for I couldn't understand what the fuss about money was. I'd tasted money, attention, fame and relationships, and become clear about the fact that none of these things could fill the void within.

Marriage was not a part of my plan or my dreams either. I knew I would renounce one day and, therefore, I thought it would be unethical to consummate the relationship. Once again, I was rather naive in my thinking. I had always seen life in black and white, believing in absolute definitions— this was good and that was bad, this was moral and that was immoral, this was right and that was wrong. How tantra used sexuality to transform and transcend the self was not something I really grasped until I experienced it first-hand when I did my first tantric sadhana of Goddess Kali. And I learnt that life was really a huge, grey sea.

Doing this particular tantric sadhana was supposed to give the practitioner a vision of Kali in a vivid dream. A process of three nights, it required invoking a mantra along with the energy of Kali in one's partner. Honestly, I wasn't sure if a short sadhana would result in anything significant but how wrong I was. Not only did I get a vision of Kali but, at the time of consummation, I felt like the only entity that existed in the entire Universe, why, I felt I *was* the Universe.

It was an experience unlike any other. Physical intimacy didn't hurt my conscience or my sadhana; on the contrary, it was incredibly beautiful and liberating. Any notion of sex or sexuality I had held was now transformed into an expression of love, a way of experiencing oneness. If I had any inhibitions about it earlier, I had none now.

I even remember sitting down later and analysing why such a beautiful act was labelled a sin in the major religions. If you had sex within a societal or religious framework like marriage, it was acceptable, but if you dared to venture beyond, it was considered a 'sin'. Who had made these rules? Some Hindu scriptures did not view sex so negatively. Nevertheless, they regarded it as a great hindrance towards one's spiritual progress because lust can easily override one's intelligence and resolve. They argued that a seeker on the path must be chaste, he or she must be steadfast in practising celibacy so they do not become prey to temptations.

I could see some sense in this, but what about the seeker who had reached the other shore? I couldn't see the wisdom in a lifelong vow of abstinence. Further, I thought it was unnatural and unnecessary. Besides, tantra offered a phenomenal way of transforming sex into a divine offering, and the only significant difference between ordinary sex and sex the tantric way is mindfulness.

Tantra insists on awareness—the awareness of each breath, thought and emotion. Sexual desire can destroy awareness effortlessly. When overcome by lust, all boundaries between right and wrong, between good and bad, blur very quickly. But tantric mindfulness turns even lust into an awareness of emotion, it transforms it into love. This is a subtle but powerful transformation because the next time any sexual thoughts occur, you don't experience a tide of lust but a wave of love. And this is no ordinary feat but an extraordinary metamorphosis: you have just successfully transformed one of the most powerful and innate human urges into a divine emotion.

My experience brought home the understanding that love was undoubtedly the most powerful emotion, a wholesome expression of one's very existence. I realized there was no other emotion as complete and as healing as love. Even compassion may be a conscious choice, but love, love is the basis of our existence and therefore strikes a chord in our innermost being.

This is why the Vedas recommended the slow and steady path to self-realization rather than an abrupt or early renunciation. They endorsed the institution of marriage, a life of moderation, the middle way. It all made sense to me now. I understood why the greatest sages were married, why even Krishna, Shiva, Vishnu and Brahma had consorts. The message here was not that marriage would bring self-realization, but that it could work as a catalyst for spiritual transformation. This is what the greatest seers and yogis had grasped.

Essentially, a householder leading a truthful life and experiencing the various colours of life, in moderation, could reach the highest state of realization far quicker than a celibate tucked away in a religious order but constantly battling with his emotions. Sex was not an experience to be fought and despised but to be understood and accepted. My views about marriage, however, did not change. Love was good, physical intimacy was good, but I didn't want marriage. I was also aware that a successful stint at tantra didn't mean I had experienced the ultimate state or that I had become an adept or even an expert meditator. One vision of Kali wasn't enough for me; I wanted to see the Divine again and again. Further, I had not yet attained the perfect stillness of the mind. During my meditations, my mind still wandered off. Nineteen years had gone since I first started meditating, and here I was, not much better than when I started.

Over time, I had become convinced that I needed a guru. Perhaps surrender to a guru was the way forward; a guru would be able to guide me and lead me to the ultimate state I so longed to reach. I genuinely believed that I wasn't getting ahead in my sadhana because I hadn't been initiated into the path of renunciation.

'Sirji?'

'Sirji?' Sandeep called me again.

I looked at him.

'We are at the railway station, Sirji.'

I picked up the backpack I had brought from home this morning and said goodbye to Sandeep. I was on my way to Varanasi. There was no particular reason why I had chosen this destination except that I thought the great tantriks lived in Varanasi, and I'd be able to find a guru there.

I first caught a train to Delhi as my connection to Varanasi was from there. In Delhi, I checked into a hotel for the night as my train was due to leave early the next morning. From my room, I called Canada and spoke to my mother and PB one more time. They both were unsuspecting, of course.

When I reached Varanasi, I checked into a lodge and went straight to bed. The next morning, I went to a cyber cafe. In addition to the individual emails I sent out to a

handful of people, I sent a common note to almost everyone
in my contact list.

The mail read:

Dear all,

*Ever since I can recall, I have ached to dedicate my life to
a higher cause, one different from just building material
wealth. With that in mind, I have always wanted to go on a
spiritual quest, a quest for the inner self. The time to pursue
my mission has come, and I must start to give it some
shape. My quest involves understanding and verifying the
truth first-hand. The truth of self-realization, that is.*

*Will I be successful? I don't know and it doesn't matter. I
will still go ahead with my plan. Is this what I really want
to do? I am only so sure. Is it worth causing my loved ones
the pain of separation? To be honest, I don't have an answer
to this question. Each one of us is unique and born with a
different purpose. The ultimate goal may well be the same;
the purpose generally isn't.*

*The moment has arrived that I must embark on the spiritual
journey of my life. For the last eighteen years, I have
waited for this moment every single day. Please take care
of yourself and each other. And know that it's only my
physical presence that is finding its nest someplace else, all
else remains unchanged.*

*From this moment on and for an indefinite period, I shall
not be contactable using any mediums of the twenty-first
century :). I am leaving my phone behind. All my email
accounts will cease to exist. And I do not have a permanent
address. Any reply to this email will bounce too.*

*I am deeply grateful to you all for the extraordinary care,
love and affection you have given me over the years. And I,*

from the core of my heart, beg for your forgiveness, for there must have been times when I hurt you with my thoughts, words or actions. If you forgive me, it'll help me travel light.

I most reverently bow to the Divine in you.

Amit

EIGHT

The Siddha

Fatigued and dehydrated after a whole day roaming around the ghats, I couldn't sleep. There was nothing more to think of where the past was concerned; I just waited for the night to pass. Eventually, I got up at 5 a.m., had a long bath and went to the breakfast area. It was closed. I made several trips to the restaurant over the next two hours but the result was the same. Somewhat flustered, I went to the reception where I found the employees sleeping; some were on the floor while others slept on the couch.

It was 9 a.m. by the time they started serving breakfast. The sun was shining bright and the mercury was already on the rise. My vision of starting my day really early was a dream as unreal as the last twenty-four hours. Manish didn't turn up until about ten. Finally, we left the guest house.

We went to a small ashram by the river called Sri Math. An old man, slightly hunched, came out and asked me where I was from and what I wanted. I told him I was in search of a guru who could guide me on the spiritual path. He asked me to follow him, telling Manish to wait outside.

I was taken into a room where two men were sitting. One of them was going through ledgers and accounts; the other, wearing white robes, sat watching. I bowed before the man in white. He began asking me questions like why I wanted to take sanyasa and whether my parents knew about it. He wanted to know where they were based, what they did, how many siblings I had, if I had a job or a business and why had I left it, what else I was after... There were other questions as well but I can't recall them now.

After grilling me for about ten minutes, he said, 'Guruji is at the Kumbh Mela in Haridwar these days.' From the outset, I hadn't sensed even an ounce of divinity in this man, but had thought that my faulty vision and shortcomings were causing me to misjudge him. The other man asked me a few more questions about my educational background and then said he was happy to see someone like me, whatever that meant. He told me I should really be in Haridwar since all the saints were gathered there. I wasn't keen on going to Haridwar or anywhere else for that matter. I was certain that God had brought me to Varanasi for a reason.

Just then, a short, fat man, also wearing white robes, entered the room. He sat on a couch and let out a loud belch. I didn't feel like bowing down before him, even though my culture and tradition required me to pay obeisance to someone in robes as they are a symbol of the dharma. I showed my discomfort at his mannerisms by not looking at him.

'Where have you come from?' he said.

'Ji, Delhi.'

'Are the trains on time these days?'

'Mine was late by four hours.'

'These rascals can never be on time, they were even born late.' And he burped again. 'I ate a bit too much.'

'Chotu! O Chotu!' He called out to someone.

A minute passed.

'O Chotu!' He raised his volume significantly.

'Ji, Babaji.' A young boy appeared.

'Why don't you ever answer the first time around? Even God appears faster than you do. Make four cups of tea.'

'Not for me, thanks. I don't take tea.' I said.

'We can get milk for you.'

'Thank you very much, but I'm fine. I just had my breakfast.'

'Make three cups then,' he said to Chotu.

'So you've had your breakfast. Where are you staying?'

'I've already been through this,' I said. I wasn't going to waste any more time here.

I offered my respects to the men, left a hundred-rupee note and got out of there as fast I could. Manish was waiting for me outside. I told him what a disaster the place had been. He laughed; I laughed too. Then, he suggested another place nearby I could explore. It turned out to be an old building and I was immediately attracted to it. Although all the buildings in this area were old, this one was particularly dilapidated. Looking at it, I was convinced I would meet a siddha here, some great yogi who sat behind its walls hidden from public view.

The main door was ajar. I knocked but there was no response. Manish pushed opened the door and we entered a courtyard. There was a giant peepul tree in the centre; its massive spread obscured a portion of the sky above. Leaves, soft and green, lay strewn on the ground along with dry brown ones. The walls were peeling; one could see the earlier coat of paint below the existing whitewash.

There was a small washroom near the entrance. I could see the floor was still wet, as if someone had just taken a bath. The tap was dripping and water was collecting in an old aluminum bucket. A mug of water sat close by, its handle broken.

Nearby, I saw a room with the door ajar. It had three single beds, while an old Naga sadhu lay on a rug spread on the floor. He looked as weary as his surroundings and was quite old, perhaps eighty. I realized he was gasping for breath. He kept pointing at his mouth and chest to convey he was unable to breathe. I had been asthmatic all my life, so I knew what it was like to struggle for breath.

I told Manish that we should take the sadhu to the hospital, and that I would pay for his treatment. Manish shook his head, saying he had been in the hospital until last week. He also informed me that there were other sadhus who lived there, and they would be back in the evening; this man was not alone.

'How do you know?' I asked Manish.

'I live around here, sir. I know this ghat and this baba too. You think anyone would leave this place unoccupied, and in this prime location?'

The other beds did look like they were freshly done, and I could see the bathroom had been used. I felt the truth of Manish's words: the sadhu was not alone. But I felt sorry for the old sadhu.

'Why isn't he taking any medication?'

'He has no money for medication and the government hospital has no facilities to help him.'

'Let's take him to a private hospital. I'll pay.'

'And what if he dies on the way? The police will say you killed him because you wanted the ashram. We'll get into trouble with the law.'

Strangely, though cruelly, he made sense to me.

When we left the building, I told Manish I needed to take a breather. I sat down on the stairs outside. I could not erase the sight of the old sadhu from my mind. Even my life could end in a similar way, and I understood that I needed to be mentally prepared for this possibility. How was I any different from the gasping sadhu? He had renounced his past and so had I.

Questions flooded my mind. No one around, young or old, renunciant or householder, seemed to have seen God: What if there *was* no God? What if I had no Maker but had just evolved over time along with other species? Perhaps my search for the Divine would prove futile and I would end up like that sadhu, wasted and abandoned.

'How can a sadhu be dying like that?' I asked Manish.

'They are not real sadhus, sir. They smoke pot all day. Some are even fugitives from justice.'

Despite this reassurance from Manish, I was unable to forget the old sadhu's face for months.

We went to another ghat after that. There, Manish took me to a temporary structure made from yellow tarpaulin. The door was open and I could see a Naga sadhu sitting on his knees, stark naked. A disciple stood near him. Wanting to meet the sadhu, I went closer to the entrance but the disciple stood up and asked me to keep away. Nevertheless, I peeped in. There was a bed on one side, some eighteen inches high, with a large lion skin spread on it. Numerous drums of food and other provisions were crammed into the hut and it was a messy little place.

I handed the disciple a fifty-rupee note. The man smiled.

'You want to have Babaji's darshan? He knows everything. Before you even got here, he knew all about you,' he said enthusiastically.

Upon seeing that Manish was a local, he threw him a contemptuous glance. I made to enter the tent. Suddenly, the baba began shouting excitedly. The disciple hurriedly told me that since the ascetic had allowed me a glimpse of him, he wanted to be left alone. I was asked to leave.

I pulled out a hundred-rupee note, which the attendant took promptly. 'Babaji, he's your devotee, he wants your blessings.' He turned to look at the holy man and showed him the money.

'Can I come in now?' I asked.

'No, that's not allowed.'

I pulled out another hundred-rupee note and he asked me to enter.

I left that very moment. Till now, I had been open to the possibility that the sadhu was an evolved being who was trying to keep me away as he didn't want to meet people. But, when more money finally opened the door, I knew this was not my destination. For me, both men were naked: one had bared his body and the other had sold his soul. I was reminded of a couplet by Kabir:

Guru jaka aandhara, chela hai jaachandh,
Andha andhe theliye, dono koop parant.

(The guru is blind and so is the disciple. The blind is leading the blind and both will end up in the well.)

I continued to wander around with Manish. I wasn't sure where I was going but I knew what I was searching for. Sometime later, a building caught my eye and I was irresistibly drawn to it. From where we were standing, I could only see the back of the structure. I told Manish I wanted to go there.

He took me up the flight of stairs to the road above the ghat and led me through another maze of streets until we arrived at the entrance to that building. There was a large iron door with grills; nestling within it was a smaller wicket gate. We knocked on this gate but no one opened it even though we could hear voices within. We waited and then knocked again.

Finally, Manish put his hand through the grill and unbolted the door from the inside. We bent over to enter and found ourselves in a courtyard. To our right was a room; inside, four young men were chatting loudly. Across the courtyard was a small temple within which sat an older man.

Seeing us, he came out. 'Where are you from?' he asked, barely managing to open his mouth as it was full of paan. Here we go again. Another interrogation, I thought. After fielding a few questions, I said, 'I want to meet Babaji.'

No one had told me that there was someone called Babaji who lived here, but somehow, I knew. Call it intuition or plain hope. Rather than answering my question, the man pointed to Manish and said, 'Who is this lad?' He scanned Manish from head to toe. I had seen men leering at women, but this was the first time I saw a man's gaze run over another man in this way. His eyes, however, were full of contempt.

'He's my guide.'

'Hmm.'

'I want to meet Babaji,' I repeated.

The young men—they must have been in their late teens or early twenties—gathered around us. The man, who I discovered was called Mishraji, twitched his eyebrows, giving an instruction to the others. Two of them started calling out. 'O Dinesh Muniji, Dinesh Muniji! O Babaji, Babaji! Dinesh Muniji!' They called out over and over again until a door opened and a man stepped into the courtyard.

Dinesh Muni was a short, dark man with a sparse beard. His hair, jet black and a little curly, was tied behind his head. He looked at me with such disdain that I gave myself a hasty once-over to see if I was dressed alright.

'He's the baba,' said the men in unison. I looked at Mishraji and he nodded.

'What do you want?' He wagged his head to put emphasis on his question.

'Not you, I want to meet Babaji,' I said.

I got everyone's attention now because they thought I already knew who the bona fide baba was since I had refused to accept Dinesh Muni's claim. My conclusion, however, was based on my assessment of his energy and attitude. It was not hard to see that he was not a particularly evolved being. He projected no radiance, his speech had no depth. His voice cut through my thoughts as he told me that Babaji wasn't there. Scolding the boys for disturbing him, he stormed off.

I sat down with Mishraji to find out more about Babaji. He explained that Babaji spent most of his time at another ashram about 80 km from Varanasi. I asked him for the address but he sounded reluctant to give it to me; perhaps he just wanted me to plead. I insisted. Finally, he gave me a vague idea, saying it was in a village called Kasvarh. 'Just get there and ask around. They will guide you,' he said.

He took pains, however, to tell me the things I had to buy for Baba. I was not to go empty-handed but take some items as an offering. He dictated a list that included two different types of sweets, dry fruits, a special pack of paan, the day's newspaper, flowers and anything else I wanted to offer him.

I was ready to go and meet Baba the very next day. Manish said he wanted Baba's darshan as well. I agreed. He had been with me for the last two days and deserved this opportunity as much as anyone else. At 6 a.m., I shook awake the people at the reception so they could unlock the main door for me. Manish was waiting for me outside. No shops, absolutely none at all, were open, so I couldn't get any of the items I was meant to buy.

We asked an autorickshaw driver if he would take us there.

'All the way?'

'And back.' I added.

'That's too far. No, I can't. It will be expensive.'

'Tell me how much? Maybe I can pay.'

'No ... it will cost a lot of money.'

'Do you want to go or not?'

'Yes, I do.'

'How much?'

'But it's too far!'

I was beginning to lose my patience.

'I'm asking you the last time. If you tell me the price, I can decide.'

'And back too?'

'Yes, I just have to be there for an hour or two, and will be back after that.'

'How many people?'

'Just the two of us.'

'Are you certain you're coming back today?'

I looked at Manish. 'What's wrong with him?'

It was early in the morning, and I was on an empty stomach. I was going to meet my guru and a simple autorickshaw driver had managed to ruin my joyous mood and dampen my enthusiasm in a matter of moments. Such is the influence petty events can have on one at times.

I looked around to see if there was any other autorickshaw available. Just then, he said, 'I'll charge Rs 600.'

I was in no mood to bargain. I nodded and hopped into the autorickshaw. Manish got in beside me.

The autorickshaw proceeded slowly and it was past 9.30 a.m. when we reached the village. Soon, we were parked outside my destination—a school building. It looked reasonably large for that small village. I was surprised to see some police constables manning the entrance. It turned out that the school was an examination centre for the BEd exams, and the police were there to prevent cheating. Apparently, cheating was rampant. The teachers promoted it by providing the students slips of paper with the answers written on them; sometimes, they even wrote answers on the blackboard. Yet, I couldn't quite understand why the constables were so heavily armed. They were carrying rifles. To confront whom? Those who brought the slips of paper?

Next to the large school building was a smaller building. I was told that this was an English-medium school that taught students till class eight. The children were singing their morning prayer, a classical eulogy of Ma Saraswati, in melodious voices:

Veena vaadini var de,
Var de veena vaadini var de,
Priye swatantra rav amrit mantra nav,
Bharat mein bhar de var de,
Var de veena vaadini var de…

(O goddess, bless us with free thought, with divine wisdom. Fill this nation with the nectar of knowledge.)

I told a policeman that I was here to see Babaji. He directed me to a small house behind the school. I walked up to the house and paused at the door, which was ajar. An ascetic sat singing the raga alaap as if in some divine ecstasy. I stood there, completely mesmerized. I had never seen an ascetic like him. Years of austerities had tanned his skin. His dark face contrasted with his pure white beard and moustache, and I felt like I was looking at a beautiful solar eclipse. His long, white, matted hair was tied in an unusual knot on top of his head. He had an unusually large forehead like tapasvins normally have. He was also pot-bellied, as if he always practised kumbhaka, yogic retention of breath, like great yogis of yore. He sat cross-legged with the detachment of a jivanmukta, a cloth covering his thighs.

He stopped singing and looked at me. His small but still eyes had a hypnotic pull; they instilled fear and awe at the same time. The first glance he threw at me didn't just see me but saw through me, it imprisoned me. I surrendered then and there. The authority in his look said he owned the place. Actually, he looked as if he owned the Universe and everything in it. I knew I had met a siddha.

As I did a full-length prostration before him, Manish came up behind me.

'Who is he?' Baba asked.

'He's my guide, Baba.'

I turned to Manish and said, 'Can you please wait near the autorickshaw?' I sensed Baba didn't like him there.

'Are you doing some research?' Baba asked me after a few introductory questions.

'No, Baba, I want to be initiated into sanyasa.'

'Why do you want to take sanyasa?'

'I have done many sadhanas. I've been experimenting and trying, and trying real hard at that, for nearly twenty years. But I haven't been able to get to that ultimate state the scriptures talk about.'

'What sadhanas have you done?'

I named some.

'Are you a Brahmin?'

'Ji, Baba. I'm a Saraswat Brahmin of the Gautam gotra.' I told him my full name too.

'Then I will teach you.'

He asked some more questions and told me to stay in his ashram in Varanasi.

'I'll see you at the ashram in two days.'

I prostrated again and offered him some money.

'When you have surrendered yourself, of what use is this money?' he said. Leaving the offering by his feet, I walked out of the cottage, feeling blessed and fulfilled.

NINE

Letting Go

It was about noon by the time we got back to Varanasi. I checked out of the guest house and said goodbye to Manish, my guide for the last two days. 'Please call on me again,' he said sweetly. 'If you don't like it here, I can help you find another ashram.' I thanked him again and headed to Baba's Varanasi ashram as I had been instructed.

At the ashram, Dinesh Muni opened a room for me. I walked in and looked around, not that there was much to see. There was no bed and no bedding, just a bare floor. And a mouldy cupboard. The room was nice and cool though. I lay down on the floor and stared at the fan. It rotated slowly and creaked as it went round and round. Welcome to self-realization, it seemed to be saying.

The hard floor was uncomfortable. I asked Dinesh Muni if it was possible to get a mattress or a sheet. Without bothering to reply, he went upstairs while I waited in the courtyard on the ground floor. After a while, he called out my name from the first floor and, when I looked up, he flung down a thin, filthy rug. It landed beside me in a cloud of dust, which triggered off a bout of coughing. Gasping for breath, I reached out for my inhaler and took a double dose.

As I waited for the coughing to subside, I wondered at Dinesh Muni's behaviour towards me. It didn't occur to me until much later that he was after money. Had I known this at the time, I would have given him some money. It would have made my life easier, and his too. To my surprise, I also learned that even though he looked and acted every bit unlettered, he was actually doing a PhD at Banaras Hindu University. It only reaffirmed my faith that bookish knowledge could take one only so far. Here he was, doing a doctorate in Sanskrit but clueless about humanity or humanism. Especially considering that the word 'Sanskrit' means one who is cultured.

There were four other residents in the ashram and they were full-time students in different colleges. They helped in the ashram chores and, in return, got free food and accommodation. Later that day, I went to the market. Rather than wasting time while I waited for Baba to come, I thought I would buy a book or two. I picked up some tantric texts, which would come in handy over the next few months I spent with Baba: they would keep me busy during the day and serve as my pillow at night.

Four days went by while I eagerly waited for Baba. I'd been longing to see him since our first meeting. In fact, not a moment went by when I didn't think of him. Meanwhile, I made another trip to the market to buy books and took Pawan, one of the students, along with me. I offered to buy refreshing lassi for both of us. He was shy at first but then had three glasses.

On our way to the bookshop, Pawan opened up and said his father owned a tea stall back in the village. Being Brahmins, it was his father's dream that Pawan become a Hindu priest.

'Is this what you want to do though?' I asked.

'Yes, but it's very hard studying and working together,' he said dejectedly. 'By the time I'm done with the ashram chores, I'm so tired I just want to sleep.'

'Have you spoken to Baba about it?'

'I can't speak to Babaji. He might get really mad at me.'

'Really?'

'Yes. Actually, I'm curious, how did you know about Babaji?'

'I didn't. Life has brought me to him and I'm sure Baba is my guru.'

'I think Babaji maybe furious if you call him just Baba.'

'His wish is my command, Pawan. I'll call him whatever he wants.'

Pawan wasn't entirely wrong because everyone else did call him Babaji. For some reason though, from day one, I called him Baba. I felt closer to him by addressing him in this way, but I did so with great love and reverence.

At the bookshop, I asked Pawan if he wanted to buy a book, but he shook his head. When I insisted I wanted to get something for him, he said he wanted a bottle of Coke. I thought it would be a good idea to get something for everyone in the ashram. We got a large soft-drink bottle, sweetened mango drinks and two packets of biscuits.

The students jumped with joy to see the shopping. Dinesh Muni softened a bit and gulped down the one-litre bottle of Coke. This treat became a regular feature. Whenever I went to buy books, I would get a couple of bottles of Coke and biscuits for them. I would also get biscuits and water for myself. It was sheer joy to be able to drink that cold water. There was a fridge in Dinesh Muni's room but I never went there and he kept the cold water to himself. Besides, he would drink straight off the bottle, so I wasn't keen on drinking from it.

Biscuits and bottled water became my preferred meal because they didn't make breakfast till 11 a.m. in the ashram. In the dhabas outside, the only breakfast available consisted of puris and samosas, both deep-fried items. I used to get up around 4 a.m., and waiting till mid-morning wasn't a good option; nor was eating puris. Of course, biscuits weren't ideal either but I had to survive.

In the evening, moths and other insects thronged the cooking area. Much to my amazement, the students and Dinesh Muni were perfectly fine with it, not making any attempt to cover the food. Even the wheat flour was left uncovered at night, and you could see scores of dead insects in the flour the next morning. The first time I saw the sight, I was shocked and didn't think it was prudent to throw away the flour everyday just because we didn't cover it at night. But they had other ideas. They would simply sift the flour, throw away the dead creatures and proceed to make the dough. I tried to suggest an alternative method a few times and tried to cover the flour at other times, but Dinesh Muni took this as interference on my part, so I stopped. I ate that food like everyone else, accepting it as part of my experience there.

There were other aspects of living there that took some getting used to. Slippers were not permitted in the ashram, not even in the washrooms, which were incredibly dirty. Squatting barefoot over the Indian-style toilet was the greatest torture I'd ever put myself through. To add insult to injury, I hadn't used such a seat in over a decade. But this situation, as it turned out, helped me prepare for life in the Himalayan forests; there, I was able to attend the call of nature effortlessly.

Within the first few days at the ashram, my feet became extremely dry and cracked. Till now, I had never been barefoot for more than a few minutes; here, I was barefoot all the time. I washed my feet every couple of hours but that didn't help.

The physical discomforts didn't bother me as much as waiting for Baba did. I was constantly thinking about him. He had said he would be there in a couple of days but there was no sign of him. I wanted to go and visit him in the village but everyone dissuaded me. 'You must wait here because that was Babaji's instruction to you.'

Finally, I couldn't wait any further and decided that I was going to see Baba at his ashram. The next morning, I put a set of clothes and some toiletries into a small polythene bag. I left late so I could buy his favourite sweets, paan and newspaper on the way. It was just past 11 a.m. when I got to Baba's ashram in the village. I almost ran from the autorickshaw to his cottage for I couldn't wait to see him. Entering his room, I prostrated before him and placed the offerings by his feet.

I thought Baba would be happy to see me again. He, however, spoke to me as if he had no recollection of our earlier meeting and no idea that I had been waiting at the ashram in Varanasi. I was as bewildered as I was disappointed but then put aside my feelings, thinking that this was perhaps Baba's way of testing me. A little later, he said, 'Alright, let's talk today.'

He asked me about my education and background. He was delighted to hear that I ran a software company and other businesses, and that I had lived in various countries. But, above all, he was particularly pleased to know that I spoke English and that I had received my higher education abroad. Subsequently, he would tell anyone who came to visit that I was an MBA from Australia.

I requested Baba to grant me permission to stay back at the ashram and serve him. He didn't respond right away. I sat quietly near him. After a while, a girl entered the room. He told her that I wanted to be his disciple, and asked her if she was comfortable with this. She nodded and they spoke to each other in Bhojpuri, the local language, which I couldn't understand. Then, Baba told me I could stay back. I let the autorickshaw go.

The girl, Nikki, used to look after Baba and cook for him. He only ate food that had been cooked by a kumari and no one else was allowed to partake of that food. It was probably linked to his tantric practice. He treated her like his own daughter, and she used to stay in his room with him. Her brother used to come and sleep with them because Baba, as a matter of principle, never stayed alone with Nikki. I was also introduced to the other people living in the ashram. There was Shesh Muni, a disciple, who was two years older than Baba. Baba's driver, who everyone called Pandey Driver, also lived there. His full name—I was one of the rare few to ask him—was Hari Om Pandey.

At the time I arrived, about ten construction workers had taken up temporary residence on the premises as Baba had commenced the construction of a third building, a degree college for girls. Baba asked me to go and rest in the nearby hut. 'Ji, Baba,' I said at his instruction. These were the words I uttered most often with Baba. No matter how absurd the instruction, if it came from his mouth, I simply said 'Ji, Baba'. And I only ever spoke if he wanted a response from me; for the rest of the time, I remained silent. I wanted to be a real disciple in every way, giving him all I had: my body, heart, mind and soul as well as my financial resources.

The holy books state that there are only two types of conversations that occur between a guru and his disciple: a guru asks and the disciple answers: or, a disciple asks and the guru may choose to answer. There is never any debate between a guru and his disciple, there is no room for answering back. This is the Eastern culture, which I respected and valued. The hut Baba directed me to was crumbling and badly in need of repair, and cobwebs covered the walls. A thin mattress lay in a corner. As soon as I unfolded it, spiders and other insects scurried out. It was full of dust; in fact, it seemed as if it was made from dust.

Pandey Driver arrived a few minutes later with a water pipe and hosed the place down. I requested him to shake the mattress vigorously to get rid of the dust as I was asthmatic. He obliged but the mattress remained dusty. I covered my face and gave it another shake. The dust got to me anyway. I took a couple of puffs of the inhaler to recover and sat down to rest. In the afternoon, Baba sent a message for me to have something to eat in Shesh Muni's room.

Shesh Muni's room was made with unplastered bricks and had a tin roof. A dirty basket containing potatoes sat in a corner, while old metal and plastic containers lay on the shelf that lined the walls. Rats, big and fearless, were jumping freely on these jars in broad daylight. God knows what was in them, for Shesh Muni only ever ate a specific type of lentil along with potatoes. He was a heart patient, so there were absolutely no spices, chillies or oil in his meals. In fact, there was just no flavour or taste in his food.

He had a single bed, which had a couple of bare mattresses; there was no bed sheet. The pillow was truly soiled, as if it had never been washed. A bunch of keys, a few broken pens without caps and some coins lay next to the pillow. An old table fan was making a disturbingly loud racket.

One corner of the room was adorned with a more modern item: a gas stove, but it turned out no one was allowed to use it except in an emergency. They cooked food on a kerosene stove instead. I had a vague memory of seeing a stove like that when I was three or four years old. When you pump it to release the kerosene, it makes a great deal of noise. Then you have to light it. Shesh Muni would later lose a part of his luxuriant white beard while lighting that stove.

A couple of days after I arrived, I discovered that Baba was getting his cottage renovated. It had two rooms, a washroom, a kitchen and a small lobby. Apparently, he was short of funds. Worried about minor expenses, he had decided to compromise on the renovation. I ventured to tell Baba that he had practised austerities all his life and there was no longer any need to do so. I suggested getting an air conditioner for his room. When he said he didn't have the money, I told him I would buy one for him. He informed me that the power outages there lasted longer than the hours when there was power, so the air conditioner would be of little use. I offered to buy a power generator. He asked me who would pay for the diesel to run the generator, and I said I could cover it from the monthly stipend my company paid me.

Baba liked my offer and gave me the permission to pay for the widgets, fixtures and all. He also asked me to get fancy lights and two small chandeliers for the rooms. I wanted to serve my guru in every possible way; had he asked me to sever my head and put it at his feet, I would have done so without a thought.

Baba also enquired about my savings and the amount of money I had in the bank. I told him the truth. I also explained that I had actually given all my money away when I left; the reason some money remained in my account was that several people had not cashed their cheques, probably due to their love and concern for me.

The next day, the plan to buy the air conditioner and other items was put into action. Baba sent for a man called Ranjay Pandey. He turned out to be a noble man who would play an important role for me later. Ranjay brought his SUV to pick me up. A couple of other people joined us, as Baba wanted them to accompany me. He stated that I was quite naive and the shopkeepers would rip me off. I said, 'Ji, Baba.'

Baba was quite pleased to see the air conditioner, power generator and fixtures for his cottage, but nothing could be installed until the renovation was complete. Thus he asked me to supervise and speed up the renovation of the cottage. I did so willingly though it was a challenge. Even while the work was going on, I had to walk barefoot on the floor, which was covered with cement, sand, dust and other construction materials. Although he wasn't living there and the place was under construction, this was his home and no one was allowed to enter with shoes on.

I cleaned my feet daily but it was the same story the next day. My heels cracked really badly and blood would ooze out. Unable to bear the pain, I once visited the construction site with my flip-flops on, but it turned out to be a bad idea as everyone thought I was being arrogant. Nikki complained to Baba though he didn't say anything to me about it.

I didn't mind the discomforts at the ashram because I was there for my sadhana, and saw them as ways to serve my guru. Was my devotion towards Baba so weak that I would crumble at the simple task of handling his construction or walking barefoot? Wasn't I supposed to rise above the slavery of my body? Hadn't I spent the first thirty years of my life mainly looking after my body? A lack of food or of the absence of respect was a small price to pay for learning the secrets of sadhana.

Anything that pushed me beyond what I was used to enduring would take me to a new level, I thought. But I was desperate to immerse myself in meditation so I could see Mother Divine and experience samadhi. I was looking up to Baba to guide me, to direct me, but it was rather hard to even get a private audience with him because Nikki was always around. She used to study in Baba's school but since he owned the school, the rules were relaxed for her. Any private time I got with him was the best part of my day.

On one of these rare occasions, I asked him, 'Baba, I really want to see God. It's possible, right?'

'What isn't possible with penance? Mother Divine is waiting with open arms for her child's loving call.'

I was moved to tears. I wanted to see Mother Divine, I wanted to play in her lap.

'Baba, I'll be eternally grateful if you can share with me any experiences you've had with the Divine.'

He chuckled and began narrating an incident. I listened with rapt attention.

'I used to be big and strong and regularly participated in wrestling competitions. Once, when I was around nineteen years old, we were three sadhus travelling to a different village to take part in a wrestling competition. On the way, we stopped by the riverside and took out our lunch. From a distance, we saw a tall sadhu coming our way, walking briskly but gracefully. His face glowed.

'I joked with him. "What's the rush, Maharaj? Are you running for alms? Come, I'll feed you."

'This angered him and he chastised me. "You have become a sadhu but you don't possess any of the traits of a sadhu."

'I teased him again. "Really? So, you tell me what a sadhu is supposed to be like?"

'He asked me to follow him if I really wanted to know. I took one of the bicycles, and told my companions that I would see them later at the competition venue. The sadhu took me to a cremation ground. There was a small temple there with an idol of the Goddess. He had me sit in front of the idol. "Now you will be able to see with your own eyes." He closed the door and it became dark inside. Lighting a lamp, he began to chant a cryptic mantra. After he finished, he said, "I'll wait for you outside." He left, shutting the door behind him.

'A few seconds later, the idol began to dance. It was a stone idol and seeing it dance made me really scared. I was sweating in fear and, if it wasn't a temple, I would have easily wet my loincloth. I stood up but the idol didn't stop dancing. I also began to hear strange sounds—the howling of jackals and dogs, flowing water, thundering clouds—and I was terrified. I sat down again but the energy continued to become more intense and unbearable. I could not take it anymore and sprang up. Without bowing, I flung the door open and ran out. The mahatma was waiting. "So? What did you see?" he asked.

'The arrogant fool that I was, I didn't want to admit that I had been humbled. "I saw nothing," I said. "Get lost, you pig, your face shows you are lying," said the sadhu.

'Falling at his feet, I asked for his forgiveness and requested him to accept me as his disciple. By lying, however, I had lost him. "I can't teach someone like you, you'd better get out of here," he said.

'I went to the cremation ground several times after that but never found him again. I sat in that temple at night, during the day, with the door open, with the door closed, but the idol did not dance again, nor did those sounds ever return.'

Baba became quiet after that. I bowed before him in gratitude for the experience he had shared with me. I wanted to ask questions about sadhana but had not the courage to break the sublime silence.

'I'm here, Bauji.' Nikki's arrival brought an end to our conversation. Two devotees from the village also arrived and started pressing his legs, which was something he really enjoyed. It was now afternoon and he always napped in the afternoons. He signalled me to leave.

❦

Daily, Baba asked me if I was actually serious about taking sanyasa diksha. 'I became a sadhu because my teacher used to beat me at school and my father used to beat me at home. I ran away at the age of nine. I'm curious as to why you want to renounce. You're educated, healthy, young and good-looking. It doesn't make sense.'

I smiled at his compliments. 'Because I want to see God, Baba. I'm not interested in material life.'

'That's fine, but I don't believe that your mother is okay with your decision.'

'No one knows where I am presently. But I had always told my mother that I would go away for my sadhana one day.'

'Guru, I won't initiate you till I speak to your mother.' Sometimes, he affectionately called me 'guru'.

One morning, I recall it was 31 March, Baba asked me to call my mother. This was not something I wanted to do but I couldn't refuse him. My mother was in Canada with my brother at the time. I called the house from Baba's phone and Ma picked up. She was overwhelmed to hear my voice. I told her I was alright and that my guru wanted to speak to her.

Baba said to her, 'Yes, my daughter, he has approached me for sanyasa. Should I make him a mahatma?'

'Babaji,' said my mother, 'He's been like this since early childhood. Please bless him so he becomes such a great soul that I may say to the whole world, "I'm the mother of a mahatma."'

Baba uttered some words of blessing and put the phone down. He was over the moon. 'I'm happy today that your mother has blessed and approved of your sadhana. Now, I'll certainly initiate you on the path of renunciation.' This was the last time I spoke to my mother during the course of my sadhana.

He began to sing a song in Bhojpuri that I didn't understand, and Nikki started laughing. Some schoolteachers came into the room and my guru turned to them. 'Today, I spoke to his mother.' Baba related his conversation and then quoted a verse from the *Ramcharitmanas*: 'Putravati jubati jag soi, raghupati bhakt jasu sut hoi. Nataru bhanj bali baad biyani, ram bimukh sut te hit jaani' (Many mothers give birth to sons, but a real mother is the one whose son devotes his life to a good cause. Otherwise, her going through the labour pain is a waste. A woman who expects welfare from a selfish son is better off being barren).

'Sarvananda. Swami Sarvananda.' He gave me the name right there.

I prostrated before him.

'I'll make you a siddha,' he added.

I folded my hands and said, 'Ji, Baba.'

'You already have everything, you just have to travel a little bit. You are born with it.'

I felt humbled.

My date of initiation, however, was postponed a couple of times. Finally, on 11 April, Baba initiated me. My head was shaved and I dropped my old clothes. I was given a set of robes and a loincloth, my secret mantra and the new name but, most of all, I was given the privilege of taking a pledge only a sanyasi was allowed: 'I hereby renounce the transient material world and enter into the life of a renunciant.'

Like butter melts on a hot plate, those words melted something within me. Just as dew drops vanish upon the emergence of the sun, the chattering mind disappeared and a feeling of great calm engulfed me. I felt like a tree after a heavy rain: new and vivified. Suddenly, I knew the purpose of my life, of this birth; there were no more confusions within. The light of the blessings of my gurus, the lineage of siddhas to which I belonged now, had dissipated the darkness of my vikara, negative tendencies.

All I needed was a vision of God, the Supreme Soul. I craved to see a manifestation of the eternal essence, but craving did not equal preparedness. I thought I was ready but the Goddess had a different view. She knew I had a long way to go, and she was right.

TEN

Ji, Baba

The day after my diksha, Baba was sitting on the floor, dressed in his black robes. He was wearing the tripundra, religious mark with three horizontal lines and a small red dot, on his forehead, and his beautiful, matted locks flowed down his back.

The door opened and the construction workers came in. They wanted their outstanding wages. A disagreement ensued between Baba and the men over the wages, and he suddenly started hurling abuses at them. I had never seen a sadhu swear and was appalled as the abuses became more graphic and ugly. Trembling in fear, the workers left quickly. I was confused. I didn't know what was more appropriate: to leave when I wasn't asked to or to sit while my guru was furious.

I was relieved when Nikki entered the room with a cup of tea for Baba. She sat near him while he drank quietly. Then he asked me to leave the room. I went out and sat beneath the shade of a young tree, my mind in a whirl. I never thought that my guru, my siddha, even knew such words, let alone utter them in rage. I was besieged by doubt. I wondered what I was doing there. Was I in the right place? Had I made a mistake?

I couldn't understand what Baba had actually accomplished in his sixty-five years of sadhana if he could still get angry like that, like any ordinary person. Immediately, I felt guilty for having such thoughts. The holy books state that a disciple must have absolute obedience for his guru. I told myself that he must have had his reasons for behaving the way he did. Perhaps it was a test for me.

'Bauji is calling you.' I looked up to see Nikki standing there. I went back into Baba's room and sat down near him.

'Don't worry about today's incident,' Baba said. 'Some people can only be sorted out with a stick. I'm an old man and I can't change myself now. Just don't be near me when I get angry because it can get very nasty,' he said before dismissing me.

I came back to sit under the tree. Although I was shocked, I didn't think any less of Baba; he had been a sadhu for more than sixty-five years, while I was just thirty years old. I didn't feel qualified enough to judge him. And where was my surrender if I doubted him? Besides, he hadn't invited me or asked me to become his disciple. It was a choice I had made and I expected myself to take responsibility for my choices. I told myself that I needed to move beyond my judgements and conditioning. Rather than imposing my idea of how my guru should be, I had to learn to accept him as he was, and to live the way he wanted me to.

While I could train my mind to think this way, my body was less forgiving. I was finding it hard to adjust to the diet, living conditions and the weather there. To make matters worse, the ashram was surrounded by golden wheat fields, and I was allergic to husk. My medication often proved to be ineffective; I was wheezing and gasping for breath much of the time. The pollen in the air blocked my nostrils and eventually led to severe bronchitis. I would have to get up every few minutes to spit out the mucus. In the mornings and afternoons, since I usually sat near Baba, I had to walk a fair distance before I could spit.

Baba used to sleep outside on a wooden bed, while I placed my mattress on the uneven brick floor near him. The mattress was just a thin layer of cotton wrapped in a sheet, and it took me a while to get used to sleeping on it. I would spend the nights dodging an insect the locals called 'kutki', which means 'pinch'. Unlike a mosquito, it didn't need to locate your vein to suck out blood; it would simply pierce your skin anywhere it wanted and leave an itchy, slightly swollen mark. Baba had a mosquito net that was good enough to keep these insects out but I had nothing. No matter how I covered myself, they would manage to get in and I would wake up with little red swellings all over my body. Showing the bites to Baba one morning, I asked if I could get a net like his. He told me to be strong.

Bathing wasn't easy either. When I bathed, my body itched as I couldn't get used to the water. I had to use a handpump to draw water from the ground, and was reminded of the handpump we used to use at home when I was a child. There was an electric motor here as well, but it was reserved to fill Baba's water tank. Everyone else had to use the handpump.

Pumping water was the least of my concerns. I was willing to do anything for Baba; I didn't want to bother him with any issues, minor or major. I wanted to be his source of joy, not tension. Besides, he had too much going on and I didn't want to add to his already full plate. He had announced publicly now that he was going to build a temple as well as a college for girls. The foundation stone for the college had been laid by none other than Baba Ramdev, the popular yoga saint. Construction had started but there was a shortage of funds. The news was spreading in the village that Baba would not be able to finish the construction unless he sold some of his land.

After I had been at Baba's ashram for nearly three weeks, he summoned me one day and shared his concern about the construction of the temple and college. He said that while he was expecting money to come through in the near future, he was completely broke right now. I told him not to worry, assuring him that whatever I had was his. Baba asked me to withdraw Rs 5 lakh from my account. I informed him that this amount might not be sufficient as we needed to order building materials as well. He told me to withdraw Rs 6 lakh instead, which I did.

Baba was pleased to get the money, and said a huge burden was off his mind since the construction work could now proceed. He felt it was a matter of honour to finish this project. I told him that as long as I was there, I would protect his honour with my life.

But it seemed Baba wasn't interested in my life. Soon, I was practically made to starve. Something strange happened just three days after I gave him that wad of money: he asked me to not touch his morning milk. I said as usual, 'Ji, Baba,' but was taken aback. Till now, he had allowed me a glass of milk every morning from his supply, and this used to be my morning meal. It was hard to take medication for asthma with just milk, but I had little choice. Luckily, I managed to arrange for a regular supply of biscuits to go with the milk.

I couldn't help but wonder what was going on. Was Baba testing me yet again? One day after my initiation, I saw him swearing. Just three days after taking the money, he was asking me not to touch the milk. I had no idea how I would survive or take my morning medication. Why was Baba doing this? Once again, there were no answers, just guilt at doubting my guru.

I tried to figure out where I could get milk, and suddenly thought of Shesh Muni. A worker used to bring him 1 kg of milk every morning from the village. When I asked Shesh Muni if I could also buy some milk, he flatly refused. 'You must learn to endure hardships,' he said. I was neither surprised nor perturbed since this place was starting to feel like Wonderland: anything was possible, and I was Alice. I pulled myself up and decided I would just have biscuits and water in the morning; I wouldn't die on such a diet.

Shesh Muni's reaction wasn't surprising for another reason. The villagers had told me that he used to be an angry young man before he became a cranky old one. Once a householder with four children, Baba had ordered him to become a renunciant when he was thirty-five, and initiated him into sanyasa so he could be in Baba's service on a full-time basis. He never wanted to live this way, but he devoted his life to his guru.

Now about seventy-seven, there was no one around to take care of him. He was in a frail condition and as good as abandoned. I felt sorry for him. He once told me that he felt ripped off and betrayed by people, and life was far better when he was a householder with a family. I could now understand why he wanted me to suffer. Suffering results in two types of people: those who become soft and gentle and do everything they can to ensure no one else has to suffer; and those who become hard and bitter, subjecting others to what they went through.

Shesh Muni's health began to worsen while I was there. He decided to go back to his wife and children for a brief rest. Before he left, he disconnected his gas cylinder and put it away but left behind a jar of wheat flour and lentils for me. The only way I could prepare meals now was on the kerosene stove, and this was a tedious and time-consuming process. I had to take someone's help. A lady who used to sweep the school agreed to cook meals for me, and without onions and garlic at that.

Onions and garlic are considered tamasic as they induce aggression and lethargy in the body. I was supposed to avoid such foods until my sadhana was complete. The lady told me that she could only come once a day, so I decided to divide the food she cooked into two parts: one for lunch and one for dinner. When I ate the chapattis, however, I felt as if I was biting on sand. We soon discovered that the wheat flour Shesh Muni had left behind was from an old batch of wheat grains that hadn't been washed before it was ground. As a result, the flour had fine dust in it. There was no way to sift and cleanse it. I was more amused than annoyed at Shesh Muni's largesse.

I managed to live like this for nearly a month. I chewed my chapattis very slowly and ate just enough to survive. Could I not have asked someone to get me some more wheat flour from the market? Well, I had brought it to Baba's attention but he told me not to complain. I was not going to die eating that flour, he had said.

Shesh Muni returned a month later, and asked me to make my own arrangements for food. He didn't want me eating in his room. I suspected he wanted to make things so difficult for me that I would run away. But I was here for Mother Divine, for my guru; everything else was immaterial.

Since I couldn't cook in his kitchen anymore, I started looking elsewhere for food. I asked the construction workers, who were only too happy to share their food with me. They ate very spicy food though; even a single bite would give me heartburn because I always ate food with minimal or no spices. Their chapattis, called tikkar in the local language, were monster chapattis. Ten of mine were equivalent to one of theirs. I would only take one-fifth of that thick chapatti and gnaw on it. Poor themselves, it wasn't easy for them to cook a meal especially for me, without onion and garlic. So, after a few days, I stopped getting food from there as well.

Now, there was no food at all, and I had to return to a diet of biscuits and water. I approached Baba and pleaded for a tiny space somewhere where I could cook my own food. He said that was not a problem; I could cook in his kitchen. He told me to get the necessary ingredients but keep them separate from his. I went to Ranjay Pandey's place, and he willingly arranged for a gas stove, gas cylinder, utensils and other items for me. I returned to the ashram quite excited. Finally, I would cook and eat to nourish my fast deteriorating body. I'd lost more than 15 kg.

When I prostrated before Baba and told him I had got the kitchen equipment and utensils, Nikki objected. Baba turned around and told me that I couldn't cook in his kitchen; he asked me to set up my kitchen in the foyer. Feeling helpless, I simply said, 'Ji, Baba.' He went on to inform me that we were leaving for Vrindavan to meet a famous swami, and I could set up my kitchen later. Before we left, Nikki told Baba that his gas cylinder had finished, so Baba asked her to use my new one till his was replaced. My kitchen, incidentally, never saw the light of the day as Baba later asked me to find some other way to eat.

We packed ours bags for Vrindavan. Several other people came along with us. In Vrindavan, Baba happened to see a nice cottage fitted with amenities and expressed his desire to have a cottage like that. He looked at me and said he wanted me to get this done. I bowed. Baba estimated its cost to be around Rs 1 lakh, but seeing the kind of things he wanted it fitted with, I knew the cottage would cost twice that. He told me I was a fool and that he would get it done in less than Rs 1 lakh. As soon as we came back from Vrindavan, he asked me to go to Allahabad to find some specialist construction workers who knew how to build permanent thatched structures. I went and met them, and they gave an estimate of Rs 2.5 lakh. Baba instructed me to withdraw around Rs 3 lakh and get the project finished.

Apart from overseeing the construction of the cottage, I was assigned other tasks as well. Routinely, Baba asked me to go from door to door in the village in the excruciating heat to promote his school. Fortunately, I was on a motorcycle being driven by someone else. Then, Baba asked me to teach English to his schoolchildren. I divided them into groups and started teaching them, but I found this physically challenging because, surviving on biscuits and water, I was always exhausted.

Baba also wanted me to oversee the construction of the college and the temple. In addition, he gave me the task of managing the finances of the school. Eventually, he asked me to assume responsibility for the entire operation of the college and school. To each of these orders, all I said was 'Ji, Baba'. I wanted to be able to put my hand on my heart and say that, as a true disciple, I did everything I could for my Baba; I wanted my surrender to be complete, else it would be meaningless.

Meanwhile, the physical environment continued to test me. One night, I was sleeping on the floor and woke up with a sharp, burning pain in my right shoulder. I used to keep a small flashlight with me as those were days of extreme heat, and all sorts of snakes and scorpions were out and about. I examined the area around my bedding with the flashlight, and saw a scorpion scurry away. The pain was extremely intense, as if someone had put a burning ember on my skin. Just then, probably because of the venom, I had an attack of diarrhoea. I knew Shesh Muni had medicine for scorpion venom. I had to go there right away but I also needed to empty my bowels. It was a strange dilemma.

Fortunately, I always slept with a bottle of water next to me since the handpump was at a distance. I had been using the fields since I had arrived, and ran there now. Though there were toilets at the school, I wasn't allowed to use them. The entrance to the school was locked at night anyway. On the way to the fields, I passed big holes in the ground that looked almost like snake pits.

After I was done, I woke up Pandey, who slept outside Shesh Muni's room, and he gave me the medication. It was a homeopathic remedy that had absolutely no impact on the pain and burning sensation. I don't know if it had any effect on the venom.

I came back to sleep on the floor. By chance, I lifted the two books I used as a pillow and saw a scorpion beneath. I didn't know if it was the same one or another. Determined to not kill any creature, I used a piece of cloth to shoo it away. If I was destined to be stung by a scorpion, I could have killed a thousand and yet another one would have come to deliver the goods. I got the scorpion to move away and did all this quietly so no one around me woke up. Anyhow, I didn't die. You can die easily if a scorpion stings you in the vein. In my case, it was kind enough; it had only kissed my shoulder.

The next day, Baba asked me to stop sleeping on the floor. 'Take a couple of benches from the school and join them together. You can sleep on them,' he said. 'Ji, Baba,' I said. I was saved from the scorpions now but the mosquitoes continued to bite. I could have covered myself properly to save myself from them, but I wasn't allowed to wear any clothes that were sewn; I had been permitted only unstitched robes. 'A true sanyasi's robes are not stitched,' Baba used to say. I was beginning to suspect that clothes, signs, symbols and even religion had absolutely nothing to do with enlightenment but, no matter what, I wasn't going to cross my guru's word.

My health and well-being, the environment and living conditions, being treated with respect and civility were not real concerns for me. My body was disturbed by them, but I knew I would train it to adjust; my intent for being there was more important. I stayed on because Baba had taken me on as his disciple and given me his word that he would teach me the secret rituals of Sri Vidya, the tantric worship of Mother Divine. He had assured me he would train me, and I had promised myself that no matter what test God put me through, I would not quit but wait for the appointed day. Without Baba's guidance, my sadhana would not progress and my desire to meet the Divine would not manifest. This was, of course, the reason why I had sought a guru in the first place.

Besides, I realized that everything I experienced here was a lesson for me. Life was teaching me every moment. One of the most important things I learnt at Baba's ashram was the type of yogi I never wanted to be.

While I waited for my sadhana to start, people began to visit the ashram to meet me. After all, I was a sadhu who had done an MBA from Australia, and the news spread. Much of the time though, people only wanted to know how to get a visa to Australia. I wished to completely do away with my social interactions but there was no way to avoid people. It was becoming increasingly clear to me that intense meditation was not a possibility here. In fact, let alone a spot for meditation, I had no place to even rest.

During the day, the sun spewed fire and I would sit in the shade of that unlivable thatched hut. And I had the scorpions as companions. But, this time, I spoke to them and told them that I would do them no harm and they shouldn't bother me either. Not once did a scorpion sting me in the hut. Sometimes, they would lose their grip on the roof and you would hear a thud as they landed on the ground, but they never breached the peace pact.

My day at the ashram started early. I used to get up at 4 a.m., take my bucket from my room and walk to the handpump. I had to pass through a narrow area dotted with shrubs on one side and trees on the other. During the night, the spiders would spin their webs between the trees and the shrubs. Unless you were careful, the gossamer web would cover your face. At the handpump, I'd have a bath, wash my robe and wear a fresh one. Using a flashlight and a small mirror, I'd apply the tilak to my forehead.

Next, I would sweep the premises as Baba would be up soon and I wanted him to have a clean environment. As I swept, I would chant the holy names of Mother Divine. Baba often had things he wanted done that day or at a later date, and I used to note down those instructions once my sweeping was done. My day was always packed. Working and teaching in the school, supervising and financing the construction of Baba's cottage, temple and college along with promotional activities for the school took up almost all my time. One day, Baba suggested I could meditate at night and work during the day. He added that I could get some sleep once school got over for the day.

When Baba handed over all his projects to me, he said, 'I'm counting on you to handle the day-to-day affairs because I can't control my rage.' What amazed me was not that my guru was busy in trivial matters—he was doing much of this for the welfare of others—but that he was so angry and bitter most of the time. Had it been anyone else, I would not have been surprised at all, but Baba of all people? After all, he was not an ordinary practitioner. For much of his life, he had practised extreme austerities. He was a Naga saint and a long-standing Sri Vidya upasak, worshipper of Mother Divine in the form of Goddess Tripura Sundari. For twelve years, he had lived with an adept called Harinam Das Aghori in a cremation ground in Varanasi, performing various rituals under the supervision of his master. He had done numerous tantric sadhanas there, as well as in the forests, in remote temples and in complete seclusion. In fact, Baba had done numerous sadhanas across the five schools of tantra.

These are different paths available to any seeker who wishes to use tantra as a rapid path to self-realization: dakshinachara, the right-handed path; vamachara, the left-handed path; kaulachara, a school introduced by the Saivites of Kashmir, which emphasizes the Siva–Sakti union; samayachara, where the primordial energy of Mother Divine is worshipped within the body above the navel and descending into the lower chakras, and sexual union with a female consort is forbidden; and mishrachara, a system that allows mixed practices depending on the state and stage of the seeker.

Vamachara and kaulachara almost always involve rituals and sexual union with a consort of the opposite sex. Dakshinichara and samayachara, on the other hand, emphasize complete abstinence whereas mishrachara permits it at the discretion of the guru. The five paths of tantra originate from the Atharva Veda, the fourth Veda.

Baba also spent nearly two decades in Vrindavan, worshipping Krishna in the tantric way. The Vedic way considers Krishna as the paramatma, Supreme Soul, and the human being as jivatma, embodied soul and, as such, is concerned with the external worship of Krishna in the form of chanting his name, singing his glories, adorning his form and reciting the Bhagavadagita. The Vedic path says the devotee merges in Krishna after death.

The tantric path is about the inner worship of Krishna. A tantrik does not find union after death attractive; he wants to unite with the Supreme Soul while in the body. This requires complete annihilation of one's societal conditioning of good and bad because a tantrik will engage in rituals that may be completely unacceptable to society. But tantra says that in order to experience and see God in everything, you must not be afraid of anything, you must face and experience all circumstances with complete equanimity. The tantric way of worshipping Krishna involves invoking his eternal consort, Shakti, through Radha.

Baba never spoke about the successes he had in various sadhanas or if he did complete them all, but he had spent his entire life in nothing but sadhana, except the last few years when he got caught up in the expansion of his ashram. He had spent eight years in Kamakhya, the foremost tantra peetha, the land of tantric practices. In line with the austerities of hatha yoga, he had also done a number of practices including pancha-agni-dhoona, where the practitioner draws a circle, seats himself in the middle and lights a fire in the four directions along the circumference of the circle; the fifth fire, the sun, burns above. Baba would do this for forty days during the height of summer from noon until 4 p.m. Pancha-agni-dhoona bestows upon the practitioner complete control over the fire elements in the body.

In the rainy season, Baba practised jala vihara, water wandering, during which he simply lived under a tree. In the winter, he did jala dhara, water flow, by sitting under a leaking pot of ice-cold water. He would sit naked while 108 pots of water would be poured over his head from midnight until 4 a.m. These methods help the seeker gain complete control over the water element in his body. Baba had also done the khadeshwari sadhana, where he did not sit down for nine years at a stretch. For more than forty years, he had been on phalahara, a gluten-free diet. Since starting his special diet, he had only drunk water from the Ganga. He was given the title of 'tantra samrat', emperor of tantric practices, by an elite congregation of tantriks.

There was not a tantric sadhana in any scripture Baba hadn't done. All in all, his accomplishments were quite impressive. With all this sadhana though, Baba remained an angry man. Watching him, I learnt a powerful lesson: religion and religious rituals and practices do not get rid of the restive tendencies of the mind because it isn't just about practising a ritual or sadhana. What matters is how they are done, with what intent and sentiment they are performed. Above all, spiritual evolution requires hard work on the self, on one's fears, patterns and conditioning. External worship doesn't guarantee one will rise above one's ego or 'negative' states such as anger, hatred and guilt. In fact, at Baba's ashram, the more religious a devotee seemed, the more rigid, narrow and egotistic I found the person to be.

Watching my daily routine here, everyone around me thought me naive and foolish. They believed I couldn't see what I was being put through. Maybe they were right.

'You are being exploited here,' Ranjay Pandey said once.

'I know, Ranjay. But the truth is that I must only look at my own karma and not the karma of others. Ultimately, in the grand scheme of things, others are just mediums or triggers for my growth; I'm simply learning my lessons here. And I want to do my duty towards my guru unconditionally.'

'Will you continue to let them exploit you like this?'

'If my sadhana doesn't start by the date promised by Baba, I'll move on. But for as long as I stay here, I will live like a disciple should.'

The truth was that the decision to stay or move on was not an absolute one for me. If Baba didn't have two extremely conflicting sides, making a decision would have been easier. On the one hand, he showed no compassion and didn't care whether I lived or died; he was completely focused on his construction projects and repeatedly broke his promises by postponing the date of my sadhana. He was a guru who swore and got angry like any other ordinary person, who rarely held a spiritual discourse or philosophical conversation.

On the other hand, he was a great tantrik who had done extraordinary penance for decades, lived a simple life and spoken fearlessly. He was the guru who had accepted me as his disciple and assured me he would guide me through my sadhana. What aspect of his was I to rely on, to believe? And what qualification did I have to judge my guru?

ELEVEN

A Dog's Life

When I was eleven years old, I had brought home an adorable puppy and named him Rocky. The owner had said it was a cross between a local breed and a German Shepherd; others said he was just a pie dog. Whatever be the case, he was an amazing animal. He was only a few days old when he came to us, and remained a dear part of our lives for nearly ten years. He had a beautiful, white chest, a beige body and a smooth, silky coat. Always alert and sharp, his erect ears would further stiffen at the slightest sound.

While walking Rocky, we had to have a piece of bread in our hands to control him. Otherwise, he would go after stray dogs or practically drag us in the direction he wanted to explore, as if he was the one taking us out for a walk. The scent of the bread was the only thing that reined him in, but not just any bread. He preferred a special type that had a currant on it, freshly baked the same day.

Whenever we ate, he sat near us, continuously staring at our food and leaving us with no option but to share our meal with him. A piece of chapatti wasn't good enough though; we had to add a little curry, pickle and yogurt. He wanted to eat exactly what we did, except for carrots. It was a simple relationship: we loved him and he loved us back.

Once, while I was sitting with Baba, Nikki brought him his food. The meal was cooked lavishly in desi ghee. The heady aroma of spices—coriander, turmeric, cumin seeds and ginger—mingled with the smell of ghee and filled the air. My mouth watered. But Baba never liked anyone sitting with him when he ate, so I was about to get up but found I couldn't. The sensations that the food aroused in me were more powerful than my will at that point. I wanted that food.

I was reminded of Rocky. I was drooling just like him, gazing at the food as if my life depended on it. I hoped that Baba, taking pity on me, might even give me a chapatti. Or, perhaps, knowing that I was barely surviving on biscuits and water, he would feel compassion and share his food with me. Perhaps my spirit of deep service during the time I had been with him might prompt him to give me a bite. But nothing happened. He wasn't even aware of my leaving, so busy was he with his meal.

I knew then that my love couldn't melt him and my service was of no value. Money I had mostly run out of. I had nothing left to give him. At the same time, I had another realization: what happens with someone may not necessarily be about who you are or what you can give but also about what the other person wants.

Basically, you can't win people over if they don't want to be won over by you. It's not that they don't want love or devotion; they do, but just not from you. They have invested their emotions somewhere else. You want to be their pet but they only see you as a dog, a watchdog perhaps. You are attached to them but they aren't attached to you. From you, they get everything too easily, so perhaps you're of no value to them. Ironically, if you don't wish to be taken for granted, if you step back, they become resentful or angry.

⁕⊱✿⊰⁕

A devotee of Baba's from another village invited him to his home one day, and Baba he said he would come. Meanwhile, the driver was absconding. He had taken leave for two days but wouldn't return until many days later. Who would drive Baba was the big question. No one at the ashram, other than me, knew how to drive. Baba refused to go in a taxi; he wanted to go in his own car, a Toyota Innova. I offered to drive him there. He said, 'You are a sadhu and not a driver. I'll take from you work that befits your robe.'

As the day drew closer, Baba raised the issue every evening. I said nothing, since he had already told me that he didn't want me to drive. Yet, I didn't like to see him worried and this was truly a trivial matter. He spoke his mind one day and said he wasn't convinced that I could drive. Apparently, knowing how to drive was a big thing in that village. I didn't know such villages still existed in India.

I had driven my Porsche at illegal speeds on the windy Highway 1 from Monterey Beach to Los Angeles and at mind-numbing speeds on the highways of the East Coast. I'd measured the roads in Auckland and Oregon, in Sydney and San Francisco, Wales and Wellington, in many of cities across the world. I could squeeze my car into the tightest of spaces and took pride in that. I changed lanes fearlessly, regardless of the number of lanes or the traffic around me. And a village road would be complicated? I was rather amused.

When the topic came up yet again, I repeated my offer to drive Baba. 'Abe tu bakland hi raha,' he said to me in Bhojpuri. He had just used a rather vulgar word to tell me that I had remained an idiot. I lowered my head. While swearing was normal for Baba, it was the first time he had abused me. He immediately softened and gestured to Nikki to bring a packet of biscuits. Opening it, he gave me two biscuits.

The day of the visit arrived and there was no driver in sight. Nor could anything be arranged as an option. This village was far, about 30 km away. Baba finally asked me to drive him. As I drove, Baba seemed pleased with my driving and said to the others in the car, 'This boy drives better than Pandey Driver.' Then he waved his hand at me and said, 'Just go slow.'

When we reached the devotee's village, we found that he had set up a tent outside the house. Baba sat on a platform that had been specially decorated for him, and I was about to sit on the floor when the host brought me a chair. I looked at Baba. He nodded and I sat down. This was the first time I had sat on a chair in front of Baba; I suppose it was allowed because his platform was still higher than mine.

Baba knew a few sentences in English. In fact, he knew the present indefinite tense thoroughly. I never heard him speak in any other tense when he did speak a little English. 'Bhhaat iz tha dipherence bhithwin Indiaan and phaaran khulture?' he asked me in front of everyone. I smiled and started answering in Hindi, but he asked me to speak in English. I was feeling rather strange because no one else knew English there. Since it was Baba's order, I spoke a few words. He then told me to come up on the platform and give a discourse on Western culture in English. I went to the dais and spoke a few sentences in English; then, I switched to Hindi and gave a spiritual discourse for the next thirty minutes. Baba gave a discourse as well. It was an interesting session.

We were invited to eat in the host's house after that. They spread a sheet on the floor and had us sit on it. We were served puris fried in ghee, delicious pumpkin curry, chickpeas, lemon and mango pickle, ginger marinated in vinegar, raita made from fresh yogurt mixed with spices, and grated bottle gourd. I found myself devouring the food; this was the first time in months I had eaten a decent meal. They also offered us mangoes, and I took one gladly. When they asked me if I wanted another mango, I nodded with enthusiasm.

While eating, I had become aware of a certain melancholy in me. Never before had I cherished a meal as much as I did this one. I had always been a picky eater, and perhaps I had taken the availability of good food for granted. I used to think that life had a grand purpose for me, and was confident that there was nothing I couldn't attain. I believed I knew better than most people. If truth be told, I had thought I was special. What had I been reduced to?

Here I was, sitting on the floor in a queue, having consumed my food, eagerly awaiting my second mango. I may have fancied myself as a monk but, in reality I was a beggar. Unlike ascetics, a beggar only takes and gives nothing in return, not even a blessing. I had nothing to offer my hosts in return. I began crying quietly and a couple of tears fell into my meal. When a mango was held out to me, I raised my hands to receive it without looking up.

Images of beggars flashed before me: worn out, ragged, dirty, smelly, unruly, drugged, creepy, strange, mad beggars. Today, I was one of them. The eagerness with which I'd waited for my food, the possessiveness I felt towards it while eating, the craving I experienced for the mango—how was my need any different from theirs? I understood why beggars savoured food they found, even if it wasn't tasty. All of a sudden, I *knew* what being one of them was like, and what having no choice actually meant.

From being a beggar, I was briefly elevated to the status of a driver when we had to go back. On reaching the ashram, Baba said he was tired and I offered to massage his legs. It was nearly 10 p.m. when he fell asleep, while I continued to massage him. After a long while, my back became stiff because he was lying on the bed with a mosquito net around him while I was bending over, with just my arms extended under the net. I don't know how many hours passed before Baba suddenly woke up and asked what I was doing there. I told him I was pressing his legs. He told me to go to bed and, turning over to his side, went back to sleep.

I prostrated before him and quickly made my bed. I lay on my back and it felt nice to stretch out. It was a quiet night, like most nights here. The sky was full of stars and a gentle breeze was blowing; the sound of the crickets was oddly comforting. It felt as if nature itself was resting. Baba was snoring softly, and Nidra Devi, the Goddess of Sleep, must have caressed me as I fell asleep in her embrace. I used to get up at 4 a.m., but I overslept and got up half an hour later.

The next day, Baba called me to his room. A few minutes later, a couple of other people joined us. Worldly talk began and I sat there, uninvolved in the gossip. Lying beside me was a book on Kabir. I had bought it in Varanasi, and Baba had borrowed it. I picked it up thinking it was better to read the words of the saint than listen to aimless talk. As soon as I lifted the book, I felt a familiar but greatly magnified pain in my right hand, just below my thumb. Before I could realize what had happened, I saw a scorpion the size of my palm crawl away. It had been hiding in the book. The other two men in the room saw it and crushed it immediately. I felt bad for the scorpion.

How come you breached the peace pact? I asked the dead scorpion. Of course, no answer came. Perhaps our agreement was territorial and therefore limited only to the thatched hut. Or may be this was the Divine will. Either way, I accepted what came my way. A bluish mark appeared on my palm, and swelled up in no time. Baba instructed Sanjay, the young man who was pressing his legs, to take me to the village hospital on his bike.

The physician there was a homeopathic doctor but gave all kinds of other medication as well. His clinic was crowded and its ambience reminded me of a veterinary clinic I had seen in my childhood. A decrepit basket overflowed with used syringes, soiled bandages, empty sachets and other medical waste.

On bare wooden beds, some patients sat while others were lying down; everyone had been put on a drip. The doctor came up to me and said, 'Don't worry, I'll give you the injection myself.' He clearly didn't want to leave me at the mercy of his assistants. He tried to give me an injection at the spot where the scorpion had stung. The syringe didn't go in properly and it hurt dreadfully. He tried again, this time suddenly and swiftly, and I nearly howled in pain. I wasn't even keen on getting the injection in the first place because it wasn't an antidote but merely a painkiller; however, it was Baba's order. Ranjay arrived soon after and took me back to the ashram.

A few hours later, I became extremely sick. My temperature soared, I started vomiting and the injected area turned purplish blue. Thank God, I had lost all appetite since there was no food to eat. Even the packets of biscuits I used to keep in the hut had been raided by field rats. I suffered like this for a couple of days. Baba chastised me for not being my usual self, for not smiling while interacting with others. Eventually, he noticed that I was really sick and scolded me, saying I wasn't strong enough. In actuality, he was getting nervous seeing my condition.

Ranjay came in the evening and saw my swollen, infected hand. And I looked emaciated, like a skeleton. The weakness was even more prominent now because of the vomiting and complete absence of food for the past few days. Alarmed to feel my body temperature, he told Baba that I needed immediate medical attention. He wanted to take me to the hospital he ran in the village.

'Take him away from here.' Baba sounded frustrated. Ranjay rushed me to his wife, Dr Vani, who was a gynaecologist and obstetrician. She examined me quickly and asked if I was allergic to anything. Then she started me on intravenous antibiotics.

'I hope it's not some pregnancy-related medication,' I joked.

She became slightly nervous. 'No, I practise general medicine too.'

She began showing me the medication.

'I was just making sure so you won't have me admitted for delivery tomorrow, you know.'

We all laughed. It felt good, human to do so; I hadn't laughed in a while.

A few minutes after the drip started, I began feeling a tightness in my chest and was unable to breathe. I didn't have my inhalers with me. It had all been so rushed that I had completely forgotten to carry them; usually, I took them with me wherever I went. There was such a struggle to push my breath out beyond my throat. I tried gasping, panting and even deep breathing but nothing worked. Dr Vani became even more nervous.

This was a village and it was nearly 9 p.m. There were no shops open at this time. Since Dr Vani didn't specialize in treating asthmatic patients, she didn't have inhalers or any other medication that might alleviate my misery. Ranjay and I decided to go back to the ashram to get my inhaler. His driver had already left for the day, and he didn't know how to drive a car, so he took me on his bike. It had been raining; as a result, we had to contend with scores of insects as Ranjay struggled to get me to the ashram. That distance of 8 km felt like an eternity and I wondered how I would survive.

Baba was sitting outside with some people when we arrived. With difficulty, I prostrated before him in the usual way. He asked me a question I couldn't even hear, much less respond to. Unable to speak, I ran to get my inhaler. After pumping more than ten doses, I felt dizzy but started to recover after a while. When I returned to the others, I heard Ranjay telling Baba about my health. I apologized to him for not answering his question. 'Go man, go away from here, first get well and then talk to me.' He sounded frustrated and angry.

Even though my life had been difficult here, it was still worthwhile because each incident was another blow to my false existence; each experience caused one more crack in the hard shell of my ego. When you are treated a certain way, eventually, you start to feel that way. I was treated like I was nobody, and I was beginning to feel like that.

I bowed again and Ranjay drove me back to his place. I took a bath and Dr Vani gave me a light meal. That was the last time I had to struggle for food. After I was discharged, she began sending me a tiffin box twice a day; it consisted of two curries, soft chapattis and a dessert. I felt nourished by the food she cooked for me with great devotion. She also sent fresh yogurt and two mangoes every day. Between running the hospital and tending to her own family, she would still find the time to cook for me daily. Ranjay travelled to and fro twice a day to deliver my meals. If not for these two angels, I might not have survived at Baba's.

Having said that, with each passing day, life wasn't getting any better. My main issue continued to be an environment that would not let me meditate. I had left everything and everyone behind because I wanted to find myself, merge with the Divine. I was tired of books and talk, and yearned for the actual experience of self-realization. But, here I was, living with a different set of people, and my goal didn't feel any closer. My family and friends were worried about me: they didn't know where I was, what I was doing or how I was. By not doing what I had set out to do, the very reason I had left them, I felt I was doing them a grave injustice.

I finally acknowledged to myself that I was simply wasting my time. Baba no longer needed me for his construction projects as they were drawing to a close. From buying stone for the temple to the construction of the cottage, I had ticked off every item on his list. He didn't really need my love or devotion either, he never seemed happy with what I was giving him. I didn't want to beg for a place in his heart; I didn't want to struggle for a place by his feet. I tried whatever I could, I did whatever he asked me, but I could not move him.

Guru Purnima, the day you express gratitude towards your guru, fell on 27 July that year. It was fast approaching, and Baba had promised to put me on the path of sadhana after Guru Purnima. I was supposed to buy some things required for various tantric rituals, but he never sat me down to give me that list. I had mentally decided that if my sadhana didn't begin the day after Guru Purnima, I would leave the ashram. Not starting it on the full moon day would have meant waiting another month. I wasn't prepared to wait even a moment longer. I knew the value of time; I had seen good times and bad times, comfortable ones and painful ones.

Baba and I travelled to Varanasi on Guru Purnima. His devotees from different parts of India were gathering there for his darshan; there was to be no discourse though. He had been a renowned tantrik in his heyday and these devotees had known him since then. Baba didn't yell at them; he didn't swear at them. On the contrary, he spoke to them happily. All day long, they sought time with him to discuss their problems.

Varanasi had no charm left for me. I asked myself if I could ever find God in these noisy, crowded streets, amidst the garbage and the chaos. Would the moment of realization dawn *here*? At times, I felt that God had long abandoned Varanasi. There was no sign of him, not in the temples, not in the priests, locals or pilgrims. Bookish, dry knowledge was what prevailed.

Baba decided to extend his stay in Varanasi, and I concluded that there was no plan for my sadhana. In the evening, he called me to his room, which was full of people, and told me to speak to a Sikh gentleman in Punjabi: he wanted me to tell him a joke. I tried but couldn't recall one. Baba wanted to know why I wasn't laughing and socializing; I remained quiet. There was nothing new to say. He knew what was in my heart. He had once told me that he had not seen God, but it was possible to do so. I had believed him. Whatever that possibility entailed, whatever it required, I was eager to do it. I was willing to give up my life for it. My present quietude upset him for some reason. He said out of the blue, 'Khushi se rehna ho toh raho, nahin toh jaake Ma...' (If you can live happily, good, otherwise go f*** your mother).

If there was a human being I had worshipped other than Baba, it was my mother. Hearing him say this untied the last knot that tied me to him. I wanted to kill myself for allowing him to finish that sentence. I didn't feel any anger towards him, only disillusionment and disappointment. I prostrated before him and came away. Perhaps Baba realized what had slipped out of his mouth, for he quickly summoned me back and gave me sweetmeats. But nothing could undo what he had just said.

The following morning, some devotees were returning to the village; the vehicle was also carrying Baba's belongings. I informed him that I needed to go to the bank, and for that I needed the key to my safety box, which was at the ashram. I told him I'd be back in a couple of hours. I had actually spoken a half-truth. I did need to go to the bank, but I didn't tell him that I was not planning to come back. It was the first and the last time I lied to my guru. From the vehicle, I borrowed someone's phone and called Ranjay. I knew his number by heart; I still do. I asked him to bring his car around to Baba's ashram in the village.

'Is everything alright?' I could hear the concern in Ranjay's voice.

'Yes, don't worry.'

I wrote a letter for Baba and left it with Ranjay. I was leaving my guru in the same manner I had left my family once. I asked Ranjay if Baba might try to harm him. He told me not to stress about anything and to do what was best for me. There was a small sum of money I had left with Ranjay, and he asked me if I needed some now. I nodded.

He quickly went to the bank to withdraw it. Meanwhile, Dr Vani cooked a tasty meal for me. As I ate, she cried. Ranjay and Dr Vani were happy to see me get out of the mess, but were sad to see me go. They weren't two people separate from me but an extension of myself; their surrender was second to none.

From the ashram, I decided to go to Haridwar by train and then further on to the Himalayas, to which I had always felt deeply drawn. Perhaps I had been there in previous lives. Ranjay got my ticket booked and I went to the bank in Varanasi. I had very little money on me and needed more. In one of my dormant bank accounts, I found there was some more cash, a couple of lakhs. I transferred the amount into my active account. Later, some of the investments I could not liquidate at the time of my renunciation because they were in a lock-in period would also yield dividends, and suddenly money would no longer be an issue for my sadhana. I got my head and beard shaved. Catching a glimpse of myself in the mirror, I could not believe it was me. It felt as if I was looking at someone else. I had become extremely weak, and was shaken and battered. But my spirit was intact.

On my way to the Himalayas, I looked up at the sky, I looked within, and I said, 'O God, O Mother Divine, if you truly exist, then please hear this: henceforth, I will never, ever knock on any human's door. Never again will I seek answers from any guru or preacher. If you exist, either show your form to me or I'll perish in meditation. If I'm convinced you don't exist, I'll go to all corners of the world and tell people not to waste their time with you; I'll tell them there is no God.'

All that I had known—and been—in the first thirty years of my life, no longer existed. Four months ago, I had cast off the various labels that defined me, but it was only now that the reality was seeping in. I knew I was not a CEO or multimillionaire or an Australian or even an Indian for that matter. I was not even a disciple or a sadhu. I understood all this, finally, because I found I was truly nothing. This is what my experience with Baba had done to me: it had emptied me of everything I had been. And only when you are empty can you begin to be filled. My cup was empty.

All these years of my life had merely been a preparation, and this time felt like a wave in the ocean, a cloud in the sky, a mist near a waterfall: it came, and just like that, it was gone. There was nothing left to lose now, not even a guru. I was ready to go to the source of all things.

TWELVE

In the Cave

I disembarked at Haridwar station in the morning and took a bus to Badrinath, one of the last inhabited regions in the northern Himalayas. Due to heavy rains, there were many roadblocks and landslides. Sitting in the bus, on windy roads, I was thoroughly exhausted by the evening. To make matters worse, I had barely eaten anything all day because I hadn't been able to find much food without onion and garlic. Admittedly, it was foolish of me to reject the food that was available while travelling. There is a fine line between sticking to your principles and losing your balance; I'd blurred it.

The bus was almost four hours behind schedule due to the roadblocks. I got down at Chamoli, 50 km before the scheduled stop, Joshimath, and checked into a hotel. Too tired to eat, I fell asleep right after a bath. The next morning, I took a shared taxi to Joshimath; about ten other people also squeezed in.

At Joshimath, I hopped into another shared taxi. A young traveller in the taxi kept staring at me. I patted my face to see if I'd got anything on it. A few minutes later, he smiled at me and I smiled back. After a while, he complimented me, saying I had a divine aura. He asked me if I was going to

Badrinath, and if I was, where I would be staying. I told him I didn't have a place in mind and would put up anywhere. He offered me his accommodation and I accepted on the condition that I wouldn't share the bed or bathroom. He agreed. Introducing himself as Dinesh Aggarwal, he told me he was a regular traveller to Badrinath and went there once every year.

Finally, we arrived at our destination. As soon as I stepped onto the land at Badrinath, I felt an inexplicable surge of joy. The spiritual vibrations here were indescribable. The sky was full of rain clouds and I was moved by its dark beauty. In those moments that I stood there breathing in the pure mountain air, I knew what it was to live in the present moment, to simply … be.

At the Badrinath shrine, I could not control my tears. Before me was a form of Vishnu—an idol. Hadn't God created this stone as well? Wasn't he in everything? I just wanted him to come out of the stone and show me his true form. Was this too much to ask?

'O Lord,' I said, 'tossed and lost, a great sinner has arrived at your doorstep. I couldn't belong to anyone, not to my loved ones, not even to my guru. I tried but couldn't win my guru. I haven't been able to win myself either. I know I can't win you but you are the ever merciful lord, please allow me to lose myself in you. You know what is in my heart, you know there's nothing else in this world I want. I beg you to either kill me or show me the way to you. You are patit-pavan, you purify the fallen ones and I'm the 'most fallen'. So, please cleanse me. You are my last refuge. I don't know how to pray, I don't know how to beg, I don't know how to live and I don't know what is good. I only know one thing: my life is useless without you.

'Test me, torment me, torture me, destroy me, my Lord,

but please keep me close, I'm worthless but I'm still yours, I don't deserve you but I won't leave you. I'm tired of this world, I'm scared of this world, do what you will to me but don't kick me away. I can't please the world anymore, show me the way to please you instead. I fully accept my defeat, I'm tired of figuring things out, O compassionate, ever merciful Sri Hari! I've no strength left, please don't forsake me but accept this arrogant and defiant pet of yours. Your Grace has brought me to the threshold, please open the door for me, don't lock me out, don't abandon me. In this holy place, in thy presence, I solemnly declare that your child won't give up crying for you till you show up.'

Suddenly, the skies roared, the clouds broke and rain came pouring down. Streams of tears continued to roll down my cheeks; the more I cried, the closer I felt to the Divine. They were not tears of pain, they were not tears of joy either; they were tears of love and surrender. The door hadn't opened for me yet but I knew I was home.

None of the pujaris in the temple bothered me, and I spent the next few hours in the temple compound, surrendering to the Grace I was enveloped in. Something had broken down in me, and I washed myself clean of everything I'd done and everything I'd been.

In the afternoon, the sky was blue and the sun bright. Dinesh insisted I go and explore a couple of places with him where I might find a suitable place for my meditation. We went to Mana Gaon, India's last village before the Chinese border, but I wasn't able to find a location I liked. I couldn't wait to sit in a cave and meditate, with every breath in and every breath out, all day and night, focusing on the divine form.

But the Universe had another reason to bring me to Mana Gaon. We met four young men there who had come to visit

Vyasa Gufa, one of the main attractions of Mana Gaon. It was said that Vedavyasa wrote the Mahabharata in this cave nearly 5,000 years ago. Dinesh began chatting with them. One of them was quiet, like me. He seemed to be lost in his own thoughts. I smiled at him, and he introduced himself as Krishna Mohan. Meanwhile, Dinesh and the other three decided to go further and see a bridge called Bheem Pul. It was said that the mighty Bheema had flung a giant stone across the river to build this bridge so that his brothers could cross.

Krishna and I declined to join them, choosing to stay back and have a chat. Quite an adventurer, he had ranged a fair bit of the Himalayas. He was due to leave for Swargarohani, a mountain summit 40 km beyond Badrinath, in two days. When I told him I was looking for a cave, he decided to take me towards Neelkanth right away. Neelkanth, named after Lord Shiva, is a mountain in Badrinath and a popular tourist site. From Mana Gaon, it took us over two hours to reach the spot, situated a few kilometres before Neelkanth.

He showed me a cave, a cavity underneath a big rock really, that was good enough for my needs. Krishna left for his trek the following day, and I ventured towards the cave again. On the way, I met a local construction worker who was willing to help me get the cave ready. Among other things, he agreed to build a wall of rocks, install a small door, cover the roof with a tarpaulin to protect me from the rains and make a small platform outside where I could bathe. I was keen to start my sadhana. According to the lunar calendar, the date was fast approaching. The worker told me that the repairs would take seven days. Every day, for the next week, I travelled to my cave to see the progress. In the meantime, I got a couple of blankets, a wooden plank, a gas stove and some other provisions.

There was another cave en route to mine. A couple of days later, a sadhu stopped me and asked if I could accompany him to his cave. I wanted to know why. He said that someone had come to visit him and wanted to give him a mantra, but neither of them knew how to write. He wanted me to scribble the mantra for him.

I said, 'I'll write it down for you, but how will you read?'

He replied, 'I know you're getting your cave ready. I'll come one day and you can read it for me.'

He was carrying two cans of water, and I took one from him to help him. I was younger, so I walked faster and reached his cave before him. I saw three people sitting inside, all in ochre robes. Two were men while the third ascetic was a lady; she looked like she was in her late forties, and had an unmistakable radiance. She asked me to come and sit inside, but I declined, saying that I was waiting for the other sadhu to arrive and didn't want to take his seat. She grinned. 'Quite some manners you have,' she said. I didn't say anything; I just wanted to write the mantra and leave.

She turned out to be a bhairavi, a female practitioner of tantra, and claimed she had acquired a couple of siddhis. One siddhi allowed her to look into anyone's past, present and future. She went on to tell me a few things about myself, which were all correct. Then, she dictated the mantra of the karna pishachini and asked me to write it down for the sadhu. Karna pishachini is a lower form of Devi that a practitioner subjugates and invokes to find out information about someone. The spirit then whispers secrets about the person in question into the practitioner's ear.

The sadhu wanted to invoke this mantra in his sadhana so he could know anything about anybody and thus impress them. It is something quite difficult to rise above the desire to be complimented and accepted. You can move beyond anger and lust, you can remain unaffected in gain or loss, but to let go the need for another's approval, what is said or thought about you, isn't easy at all. It takes great insight and a strong sense of self-worth to move beyond this need. Anyhow, I wrote down the mantra for the sadhu.

While we were sitting in the cave, it began raining. My reality hit me all of a sudden. I was finally in the Himalayas, in the company of mendicants. And I was free. There was no struggle of any sort, no worries of the past or the future: this is where I had always wanted to be, and each moment was unadulterated joy. I felt like a sadhu for the first time. In my devotional sentiment, I sang a full-bodied stuti to Mother Divine. The bhairavi was delighted to hear it.

'I want to impart to you a special knowledge, a supernatural power I have,' she said.

'Thank you, Ma, but I don't want any supernatural powers.'

'Take it, son, you are the first and the only one I'm giving it to.'

'Thanks, but I really don't want it.'

'Give it to me, Mataji,' one of the other sadhus spoke. 'I want it.'

Ignoring him, she continued. 'You have to take it now. I know you'll never misuse it.'

'I don't want to waste any time on anything else. I just want to see Mother Divine.'

'But she was already here! Didn't you see that when you sang, a butterfly flitted about you and then sat on your robe? That was her; it was her indication, a clear sign.'

'Ma, with all due respect, I have been invoking the Divine with mantras for nearly twenty years, and I am sick and tired of signs, signs and more signs. If she, the Empress, is real, why doesn't she give me her darshan? Why doesn't she manifest her form in front of me?'

There was complete silence in the cave. Outside, you could hear the rain falling on the leaves. Between that sound and the absolute stillness within, there was nothing else. Then the bhairavi smiled.

'Is that so?' she said softly. 'Granted.'

Her words gave me goose bumps. She continued. 'In less than one year, you will have her most unambiguous vision, and then you will visit the tantra peetha, Kamakhya. There, I have said it.'

'Really? I'll have a complete vision?'

She said, 'Indeed, if you won't get her vision, who will? Indra's seat will shake if the Mother refuses to manifest for you.'

In the moments that followed, I ceased to even hear the raindrops; time stood still. I felt I had lost contact with my corporeal life, with the world around me. For the first time, someone had given me the confidence that it was possible to see God and that I would get her vision. Her words elevated me to a whole new level of being, as if a million darts of faith and devotion, of confidence and conviction, had pierced through every pore of my being. I decided that even if my body perished in the process, I would meditate day and night and do whatever it took to see God.

She went on. 'Now, you must do a forty-day sadhana, which I shall teach you. On that mountain,' she said, and pointed to a distant mountain, 'Gandharv, the celestial musicians, will come to you and you will hear their performance. If my words turn out to be false, may I be a leper for the rest of my life.'

'Thank you, but I really just want to do my own sadhana. I don't want to devote forty days to hearing celestial music.'

'You are my rebellious child.' She laughed softly. 'You can do this sadhana with your primary sadhana. No more arguments.'

She taught me privately and explained that the sadhana allowed the practitioner to experience other planes of existence. It had taken her three decades to master this. She said she could also teach me how to do vayu gaman, travel through the air. I told her I wasn't interested because I only wanted to spend my time in meditating on Mother Divine, not hankering after siddhis or supernatural powers. Besides, I told her, if I needed to travel through the air I would simply buy a plane ticket.

Coincidentally, I would end up buying a plane ticket a year later to go to Kamakhya. It is said that some people's words should not be taken lightly. The words of those who practise truth are like potent seeds in a fertile ground. They don't go waste but manifest sooner or later. Everything the bhairavi said would turn out to be true. I asked her where was she from. She mentioned that she lived near the cremation ground in Kamakhya. I wanted to see her after my sadhana was over, and asked her how I could find her. She didn't have any contact number and told me to simply enquire about her when I got to the cremation ground. She asked if I had any helper to assist me with my daily chores. I replied in the negative, saying I wanted to be on my own.

'You have become a sadhu but you are a king and will always remain a king,' she said warmly. 'You will always have a helper.' Then she added, 'Your guru will burn in hell till eternity.'

I was surprised by her sudden comment; I had not told her about Baba. Also, no matter what he had done to me, I had never allowed anyone to speak ill of him because he did initiate me.

I kept quiet. She said, 'You are too simple. You don't know what was going on there. Yet, because of your simplicity and your childlike heart, you will play in the lap of the Mother.'

She gently caressed my face. 'Kasturi kundali base, mrig dhoonde ban mahi' (The musk is in the deer's stomach, yet he is frantically searching for it in the woods).

After a long pause, she said, 'Your sadhana is complete, my son. You already have everything; you need not torture yourself any longer.'

I listened to her intently. She had a magnetic energy about her, an extraordinary pull. She also predicted the tantric sadhanas I would do in the future, both vamachara and dakshinachara.

'Vamachara? I have no such plan, Mother.'

'You will have to do lata sadhan, mahacheen kram, kaulik sadhana and mahamudra.'

She laughed, for she had just named sadhanas that required a female consort.

'But I'm a renunciant!'

'So?'

'How can I practise the left-handed path of tantra?'

She started laughing again.

'Why not? You think the success in your first sadhana was a coincidence?' She was referring to the tantric sadhana of Kali I had done with a woman a few years ago. I was startled, and wondered how she could have known this.

'Why, wasn't your guru a tantrik?' she continued. 'Besides, the differentiation between a sanyasi and a tantrik that you speak of is merely bookish. Your definition will change the day you experience your own truth. Next year, you'll have the vision of the Goddess and will receive your highest tantric initiation. You will know the next step automatically.'

'But what if I decide I won't do left-handed sadhanas in the future?'

'It's written in the book of fate,' she said. 'Anyway, you should do what you've come here to do. Many esoteric sciences have disappeared and you have to bring them to life. You renounced this world to be free, now why are you fettering yourself?'

I bowed before her. 'Swami will do whatever Mother Divine wants him to do,' I said.

On 9 August, I retreated into my cave. It was freezing because the stones on the walls and floor were not only damp but covered by tarp, so they retained their coldness and moisture. There was no sunlight in the cave, and I didn't have any sewn cloth to cover myself with. Our body has a natural mechanism of maintaining heat. But, for this mechanism to work effectively, the body ought to be covered. Fabric that is stitched helps retain body heat. I wasn't wearing any such clothes as I was still adhering to Baba's instruction of wearing loose robes. He had permitted knitted materials, although I couldn't see the rationale behind this. Luckily, I had bought a flimsy shawl on my first day in Badrinath, which would prove rather handy while I lived in the cave.

On the second day there, I felt low on oxygen. I used my inhaler but it didn't help. In the afternoon, I went down to the market and got portable oxygen cylinders. Since it was late by the time I was done, I spent the night there and came back to the cave the next day. This would be the only occasion I would leave the cave in the two months I lived there.

My intense meditation routine started two days later. I meditated almost all the time except between noon and 4 p.m. During this time, I kept my door open. I started eating one meal a day, at about 11 a.m.; it consisted of thin wheat noodles boiled in milk. There was someone from the village who used to keep a bottle of milk outside my cave every morning.

Soon, I established a routine for myself. Each day, I bathed outside during or before sunrise, and the water was freezing. But whether I had to bathe with icy water or rub snow into my skin, I wasn't bothered. For that matter, what I ate, or if I ate at all, wasn't a concern any longer. My time at Baba's ashram had made me quite indifferent to such situations.

I would spend forty-five minutes daily in chores like cooking, washing dishes and fetching water from a nearby river. I always felt such tasks were a waste of time because they took me away from my sadhana. One day, I thought it would be nice if I had someone, a few hundred metres away, to do these things for me. I could eat my meal at his place, and focus on my meditation the rest of the time.

As the days went by, the locals as well as the pilgrims visiting Badrinath heard about me, and began visiting my cave to pay their respects. I was happy during the days of torrential rains because no one could visit me then. On sunny days, however, I had visitors every afternoon. I wasn't fond of these interactions, so I began thinking of inhabiting a more remote place for my meditation.

Even though I had never been to Odisha, an image of Jagannath Puri came into my mind. I longed to meditate by the sea and thought Puri would be the best place to do so. I envisaged meditating and living on an isolated seashore; it sounded idyllic. The next afternoon, a voice within instructed me to go outside. I obeyed, and spotted a man standing in the distance. I waved at him and went back into the cave without waiting for him. I had done what the voice had asked me to do, and now it was up to God to take it forward. A few minutes later, a man arrived at the cave. He was wearing white, which indicates that he had been initiated as a brahmachari, a celibate monk, by his guru. He told me there were three other friends with him, but they were waiting a little distance away.

'You are from Odisha,' I said to him as soon as he sat down.

He looked mystified and asked how I knew.

'Just like that,' I said.

'Who's Krishna Das?' I asked after a long pause.

'Why, he's my brother. How do you know his name, Swamiji?'

'Just like that,' I said.

'No, Swamiji, no one can tell names just like that. I want to be in your service.'

I then shared with him my desire of doing sadhana by the sea. We agreed that after my stint in the cave, I would meet him in Puri. His name was Pradeep Brahmachari, and he gave me his brother's phone number. Like me, Pradeep did not have a phone. It was already 4 p.m. and I had to close the door of my cave, so I asked him to leave.

≈≈≈

The two months in the cave were unlike any other place I had ever lived in. Practically, there were many challenges. It was extremely cold and any surface I touched was icy. Rats were a nuisance; it didn't help that I lay just 4 cm above the ground. One of the side effects of meditation is that your sleep becomes light. This is because you learn to maintain a state of consciousness, of awareness. So, as the rats scuttled about, they would wake me up. Yet, all this was a small price to pay for living in the Himalayas.

Meditation was almost effortless in this spiritually charged land. Thoughts didn't arise as much, and the mind was stable and serene. Moments of deep absorption would arise naturally. In addition to my own sadhana, I did what Bhairavi Ma had told me and, much to my own surprise, I did hear celestial music multiple times, exactly as she had predicted. It reaffirmed my faith in the existence of another dimension. Many a time, at night, during the day, at dawn, at dusk, I specifically stepped outside to see if it was just the blowing wind that produced this sound; however, that was not the case. I could hear it clearly both inside and outside.

On the night of 23 September, a full-moon night, I completed my forty-day sadhana. Bhairavi Ma had instructed me to do perform a yajna on this night. All mantra sadhanas require a fire offering at the end to mark the completion of the sadhana. This is done to express gratitude to all the seen and unseen forces, to the five elements and to every entity in creation.

I stepped outside the cave after finishing my evening meditation. A clear sky with no clouds, like a quiet mind with no thoughts, gave the impression of a bejewelled parasol adorned with stars. Due to the torrential rains, ceaseless like human desires, the rivers were full and the surroundings lush and green. Under the soft moonlight, the waterfalls—sheets of molten silver—dropped down to the ground in complete surrender, and the earth received them with tremendous love, much like a true devotee who drops his ego and merges with the Guru. The stars felt so close that you could extend your arm and touch them. Of course, this was an illusion like the pleasures of the world. The full moon had lit up the Himalayas softly, and shone quietly in the star-studded sky, at peace with itself, just like a realized person.

While I was absorbed in my meagre attempt to capture in my mind the splendour and grandeur of everything around me, I heard wild dogs barking. There was possibly a snow leopard or tiger nearby, and an instinctive fear sprang up in me. Half a minute or so must have passed before I reminded myself that if the death of the body was destined at that moment, it would not require a tiger to kill. Suddenly, the Himalayas were luminous again, their beauty restored.

Pleased at the favourable weather conditions, I created a little firepit outside the cave to start the yajna. The dogs had gone quiet and silence prevailed—a deafening silence. With my mind quiet and consciousness channelized, I spread my mat on the ground and placed the yajna materials beside it. The chill in the air had penetrated my flimsy shawl; other than that, I wore just a loincloth. I had blankets in the cave but I chose to continue with what I had on. I sat down.

After the purificatory rituals, I started chanting the Vedic hymns as part of the initial invocation required for the yajna. I felt deeply in touch with my soul as I chanted mantras and poured oblations into the fire. With each oblation, the fire would rise a little. This was probably due to the camphor and other materials in the offering; to me, however, lost in my own world, it felt as if Agni was accepting every single offering I gave.

After completing the yajna, I had to go down to the river. Walking from the cave to the river was a tricky job as the path had innumerable stones of various sizes lying about, and the grass was slippery with dew. The moonlight was a poor substitute for a decent flashlight, and my little torch was less than useful. Anyway, I walked the distance of about 300 metres safely.

After performing ablutions by the river, I stayed there for sometime, allowing myself to be one with the supernal sound of the river that roared past in the quiet mountains. Eventually, I made my way back to the cave and sat outside for a while longer. My body was numb and cold, my mind quiet and peaceful and my consciousness flowed like the river I had just seen. An insight began to emerge on the horizon of my mind: beauty does not lie in the eyes of the beholder but in the *mind* of the perceiver. The cleaner the mind, the greater the beauty; the quieter the mind, the more enduring the experience. An empty mind is not a devil's workshop; on the contrary, a passionate mind is, because a mind full of passions is often restless. An empty mind is but a divine blessing, for it is free of thoughts—a rare but coveted state for any yogi. If the mind was an ocean, a passionate mind would be tidal while an empty mind would be a calm, still ocean.

I stepped into my cave, which felt cosy after the extreme chill outdoors. It had got very late and I had to get up just a few hours later. I lay down on the wooden plank to protect myself from seepage as well as the damp, cold floor of stones, and covered my body with blankets. Mice, like any other night, came that night too. They must have grazed me as they ran past, and made noises that would transform the small cave into a playground. But I slept unaware and unaffected. Everything was in order for the mind was absolutely quiet.

Where else could I have experienced such divinity? With all the challenges they offer, be it through the harsh elements or through the difficulties of living in the wild, the Himalayas, for inexplicable reasons, remain the ultimate place for meditation. The Hindu tradition says that over the course of thousands of years, some of the greatest saints have meditated in the Himalayas, and you can still feel their divine energy there. I don't have any proof, nothing to substantiate this claim. But, having been around the world, I can say without the slightest hesitation that when it comes to spiritual vibrations and a certain purity, there is no other place in the world like the Himalayas.

The mountains of Switzerland, the meadows of New Zealand, the landscapes of North America, the beaches of Australia, the sunny coasts of the Caribbean, the French countryside ... I've been there, and these places simply don't match the divinity that runs through the Himalayas. Those places offer exquisite beauty, no doubt; at times, they surpass the Himalayas when it comes to magnificence, unobstructed views, even the quietude and solitude. But the help you get on your spiritual journey from the indescribable and unseen forces of the Himalayas, you cannot get elsewhere.

⁂

Before I knew it, two months were up. I descended from my cave and offered my prayers at the Badrinath temple. I thanked the unknowable and divine powers for letting me stay and meditate there. Looking back at this time, I saw that I was able to experience brief periods of absorption but hadn't achieved the complete cessation of thought. During my meditations, my mind would still wander off, and I would not be able to concentrate on the object of my meditation. Sometimes, people would visit me in the afternoon and the conversation would play in my head later that evening when I was meditating.

Physical austerity was only a small part, an insignificant part of my sadhana. What mattered far more was the mental discipline. I had to tame my mind. Completely. In extreme tranquility and concentration, I wished to witness a manifestation of the Divine.

I had to go beyond the chatter of the mind to have a true experience of samadhi. I knew I had to call Mother Divine in a state of *perfect* stillness, else I couldn't possibly hope to have her vision. I would have to increase the duration and intensity of my meditation and take my sadhana to the next level. I had to be in a place where no human being could approach me, where, day and night, I could remain immersed in deep meditation.

Until now, even though I had been meditating, the fire that I received was that of a matchstick. It was too little and too brief to give warmth or light, it wasn't enough to burn innate tendencies of my mind. To rise above my own mind, to completely burn my mental and emotional afflictions, I needed a wildfire, the fire of penance.

The scriptures clearly mentioned that with devotion and concentration, one could see the unseen, know the unknowable. This was my benchmark and the validation I was looking for. The Himalayas had given me a glimpse, but I wanted the full picture. By hearing celestial music and by experiencing intermittent periods of absorption, the Divine had only touched me. I wanted the full embrace.

THIRTEEN

The Himalayan Woods

As planned with Pradeep in the Badrinath cave, I travelled to Odisha to find a secluded spot by the seaside. Over the next ten days, Pradeep and I ranged more than 500 km. There was never an uninhabited stretch of more than a kilometre or two for we encountered fishermen everywhere. We hired autorickshaws for entire days and also went out on a motorcycle to explore the area, but had no luck. We even went to distant towns by train but I couldn't find a place suitable for my sadhana.

I prayed at the Jagannath temple, and then told Pradeep I was heading back to the Himalayas.

'Please, Swamiji, I've found someone like you with great difficulty and I don't want to lose you.'

His eyes filled with tears.

'I must leave for my sadhana, Pradeep. Once I am done, I'll establish contact with you,' I reassured him.

Leaving him behind, I went back to the Himalayas to continue my search. I had heard of the Anasuya temple near a village called Mandal, and decided to go there. I got down at Chamoli, took a shared taxi to Gopeshwar and then another from Gopeshwar to Mandal. From Mandal, there was a trek of 4 km to the Anasuya temple. When I reached, two local boys, Babloo and Vinod, who were the sons of the temple priests, struck up a conversation with me. I told them I was searching for a place to meditate, and preferred a cave. They told me about a cave called Atri Muni Gufa, and agreed to take me there. It was a lovely site but not as remote as I would have liked; pilgrims to the temple often came here as well.

Meanwhile, something else occurred to me. As soon as I had arrived at Mandal village, before proceeding to the Anasuya temple, I had noticed a small, white structure in the far distance, high up in the mountains. Apparently, it was a tiny temple belonging to the local deity. The villagers told me that no tourists were allowed there because it was a wildlife sanctuary; only locals could go there to find firewood and hay for cattle. Some shepherds did have huts there, but these were old dwellings, built long before the area was marked as a reserve forest by the government. Upon asking, I was told that the huts remained unoccupied during the winter since the place was uninhabitable at that time. A deserted location. Dense woods. This was music to my ears.

I asked Babloo and Vinod if they could show me this hut. They informed me that it would take one full day to go and come back as it was a steep hike of 6 km. They recommended I use the cave, saying it was a more practical option. Reluctantly, I agreed.

I paid them some money to buy a wooden plank, some provisions and a tarpaulin to cover the mouth of the cave, which was 5 feet wide. Then I went back to Haridwar to pick up my bag. I had left it behind because I didn't know how long it would take me to find a place, and I didn't want to carry my backpack around. But it wasn't just for this that destiny sent me to Haridwar.

I had left my bag with an elderly sadhu I had met in Badrinath. His name was Swayam Prakash Brahmam and he was originally from Tamil Nadu. Presently, he lived in Kankhal near Haridwar. He was protective, even possessive, about me.

When I reached his place, another young ascetic was there with him. He seemed a quiet, sincere seeker.

'You can have a darshan of Mother Divine,' I said, when I saw him looking at the floor.

His eyes lit up, and he said, 'Really, Swamiji?'

I nodded. 'You worship the Goddess.'

He had never told anyone this. He came and sat near me and told me his name was Swami Vidyananda.

'Please say something more,' he said.

I asked him to meet me the following day.

Swami Vidyananda came back the next day and said, 'Swamiji, I thought about you the whole night. I couldn't wait for dawn, I couldn't eat; I was so excited. What sadhana should I do for Mother Divine's grace?'

'Self-purification.'

'Will you accept me as your disciple and guide me?

'We don't need to label the relationship. I'll see you when I get back from the Himalayas.'

His big eyes welled up.

'Don't worry, Swamiji, I'll hold your hand and take you to Mother Divine,' I assured him. 'This is one swami's promise to another.'

'I saw in your eyes yesterday that you knew everything but I was scared to talk to you,' he replied softly.

'No one knows everything, Swamiji. But I did see that you were special, a true devotee, and wanted to help you,' I said.

I asked him not to accept money or any material gifts from anyone, and explained that I would take care of his necessities for the rest of his life. He was no ordinary devotee. For years, he had cried for God, searched desperately for a guru and even kept an idol of Mother Divine on his chest every night while sleeping. He'd fasted, he'd chanted, he'd meditated, he'd done everything anyone had ever told him to. If someone deserved blessings, guidance and direction, he did.

I travelled back to the Anasuya temple, this time with my bag. At the temple, I met with Babloo and Vinod and insisted on seeing the hut on the top of the mountain range. A strange force was pulling me towards it. Vinod finally agreed to take me there. We crossed several streams and walked through dense forests full of tall deodar trees. At times, hearing a sudden sound from behind a shrub or a tree, he would abruptly stop.

'Why the sudden halt, Vinod?'

'It could be a bear or a tiger, Maharaji,' he said, 'we have to be careful.'

I couldn't be certain whether it was because of my stint in the cave or my burning desire for God, but I didn't feel any fear.

The trek was a bit arduous, particularly because I had no proper shoes, only slippers. But the woods had a hypnotic quality about them, and I enjoyed the walk. It took us nearly three hours to reach our destination, and it was love at first sight. The place was extremely quiet and remote and there was a water source nearby. Around the hut, there was an open field dotted by tall trees, behind which stood the majestic mountains. There was even a small temple not far from the hut. I couldn't have asked for more. I also discovered there was another hut at a distance of about 200 metres, which would be ideal for Pradeep.

I had a message sent to Pradeep via his brother, since that

was the only phone number I had. I wanted Pradeep to get in touch with me immediately. Even if he was to leave for Mandal right away, it would take him three days to reach me. I had to start my sadhana on 19 November, and there were just three days to go. Further, we had to be in the hut a day earlier so that I could start on time. Otherwise, I would have to wait another month for the right date according to the lunar calendar.

In the rituals of tantra, the lunar calendar plays a crucial role. Just like your vote only counts if you vote on polling day, not a day earlier or later, some sadhanas can only be started on certain days. This information is never fully documented in the scriptures to prevent abuse or misuse of the powers a seeker gains by way of mantra siddhi; it is usually communicated through an oral tradition.

Currently, the chances of Pradeep making it in time were unrealistically optimistic at best, and downright unrealistic at worst. However, when we called Pradeep's brother, he informed us that Pradeep had left for Haridwar two days ago. He said he would pass on the message to his cousin who was supposed to receive Pradeep at Haridwar station.

Pradeep was already coming towards the Himalayas even though he had no clue where I was. Interesting. The Universe had planted a thought in his mind before I had even seen the huts. I wondered what he had been thinking. What if I had not made contact? How would he know where I was? The fact was, the Universe knew.

'Maharaj!' said Babloo, 'with your sankalp, you already had Pradeep start out two days ago!'

'Oh no, Babloo, not at all. I didn't do anything, I didn't even know two days ago. This is how the Divine operates.'

'What a miraculous coincidence then.'

'We use this word a bit too casually, you know.

Coincidence generally means the occurrence of something in a striking manner without any causal connection. The truth is there are no accidents in the play of nature. The creation of this universe, our galaxy, the species of flora and fauna, the five elements, a near perfect ecosystem—none of this is a coincidence. Rain, storms, mountains, seas, trees ... they are all there for a reason. Nothing is non-causal; everything supports a bigger cause.'

'You already know so much. I'm intrigued as to why you still need to meditate. Why do you want to go through hardships in the woods?'

'Like everyone else, Babloo, my mind can be talkative at times. It has been conditioned and has lost touch with its natural, pure state. I want to rise above this conditioning, above the intellect. I also have baggage to let go off so that I may become light enough to fly and see the world from a different angle.

'I no longer wish to be a balloon filled with water, heavy and unable to fly. If anything, I want to fill myself with unconditional love and light. Everyone is a balloon, you know. Some are full of waste water, while others carry a certain fragrance. When circumstances or situations prick them, they burst. But it's only when a balloon bursts that we really know what's inside. Some stink when they burst, they let out foul words, they perform despicable actions; others emit a deep fragrance. I want to empty myself so I can fill the balloon of my life with love and light, with compassion and humility.'

Pradeep arrived in Haridwar the same night. His cousin picked him up and they contacted Babloo right away. The following evening, Pradeep was sitting right in front of me. He had a fever, yet he had chosen to come. The next day, Babloo went to the town to get provisions while Pradeep and I travelled to our destination.

My hut, at an altitude of 9,000 feet, was near the edge of a cliff. You could step out and, at a distance of less than 15 feet, fall over the edge. The hut had probably been used for cattle; it wasn't really designed for a human being. The entire space was approximately 30 feet long and 10 feet wide.

The hay on the thatched roof was old and mushy, while the walls had numerous holes. One of the walls was made of concrete and tilted at an odd 70° angle. Boughs of trees several feet long had been placed on the outside of that wall to prevent it from falling. How that wall withstood the massive and merciless Himalayan storms was beyond all reasoning. Perhaps it goes to show that when you are willing to bend a little, you may look out of place but you will survive. The remaining three walls were made of planks of wood laid next to each other in a haphazard way. Due to the tilting wall, a gap had formed between the roof and that wall. As a result, during the rains, water would come in through the gap. In a corner of the shack, there was a little enclosure that could house six to eight cows, and that is where I used to bathe.

I began my sadhana on the night of 19 November. It was a beautiful night sky. A cold breeze was blowing gently, and the woods were quiet. When I started meditating, I knew that coming here was the right decision. The peace was profound. Only the locals knew this place and they rarely came this way because it was right in the middle of the jungle. Even people like Babloo and Vinod, who were born and brought up here, had never been in this part of the forest.

Initially, I meditated for a straight stretch of ten hours, starting at 2 a.m. I also meditated for shorter sessions ranging from 2 to 7 hours. At noon, I would go out to eat in Pradeep's hut. This was my only meal in twenty-four hours, and consisted of three thin chapattis, lentils and, occasionally, a bowl of vegetables. It was due to Pradeep's exceptional organization that we managed to get any vegetables. He had tied up with a villager to have the vegetables delivered once a week. This was not all though; Pradeep was a great help to me in other ways too. I used to perform a yajna after my meditation every day, and he would stock enough wood for me in advance. Every four days, he would also fill my bucket and another vessel I used for storing water.

After an hour in Pradeep's hut, I would go back to mine. From 1 p.m. to 9 p.m., I would practise contemplative meditation. Meditation is predominantly of two types: concentrative and contemplative. In the first kind, you build your concentration. In the second, you use it to reflect on the nature of reality and your own existence. Contemplative meditation gives birth to insight, and it is this insight that changes how you see and interpret the world around you. Deep concentration leads to samadhi, and deep contemplation allows you to maintain that state while dealing with the challenges of the world. I alternated between the two types of meditation.

My sleep reduced drastically as a result of the intense meditation. The highly uncomfortable living conditions and the single frugal meal I had also affected my sleep. I would sleep from 9 p.m. to 1 a.m. A bath with ice-cold water would follow, while chilly winds blew through the holes and cracks in the walls of my hut. At 2 a.m., I would start my meditation and sit till noon the following day.

However, as my mind began quieting down, I could not sleep for even the four hours I used to. Reduction in sleep is a natural outcome of correct meditation. Why do we even sleep at the first place? It's because our body and mind need rest. The vital energies flow naturally in a restful state, making us feel refreshed after a deep sleep. Meditation does exactly the same: it rejuvenates your body and mind. I changed my routine and now slept from 9 p.m. to 11 p.m., after which I would begin meditating.

A few weeks later, I began sleeping from 7 p.m. to 9 p.m., and brought my meditation forward by yet another two hours. So, I meditated for thirteen hours straight. Eventually, I gave up on those two hours of sleep as well. In a trance-like state, my mind stopped asking for sleep, and my body never sounded an alarm suggesting it needed sleep. Then I realized that I had to give my body and mind some rest. So I forced myself to nap for two hours in the evenings.

I used to sleep on three wooden planks laid next to each other on the floor of the hut. The one in the middle had bent due to prolonged sitting. There was a thin mattress, no thicker than three cotton sheets, that I had laid over the planks. And I had a quilt. This was my bed. I was at the same level as the insects and rodents that came into my hut.

꙳ᘒ꙳

You would think that living in an isolated mountain abode, miles away from habitation, I would find the deepest silence. Yes and no. While there was no artificial noise, no traffic, TV or human beings, there were plenty of other sounds that made it hard for me to meditate. Most notable were the birds. They would chirp for hours every night; I presume they were attracting the females. One poor male would sing continuously for 20–30 minutes, take a break of a few seconds and call out again with the same fervour. An hour or two later, some female would respond, the communication would start and the male would fly out to the female. None of this was actually visible but I could make out what was happening from the way their songs travelled.

I had no problem with the amorous nature of these birds. After all, sex, and not religion, is the basis, cause and consequence of evolution. Only, their loud noises were a great distraction in my meditation. Imagine you are trying to concentrate in the deafening silence of the night in the snowy Himalayan forests, and a bird starts to make a sound: 'Tnk, tnk, tnk, tnk, tnk, tnk ...' I even found myself praying sometimes, 'O Lord, if you exist, please send this fellow a companion. Have mercy on him. He's desperate.'

Over time, I learned to ignore these distractions. Perhaps this was all part of my sadhana. Birds continued to sing at different times and at varying pitches, but they eventually ceased to bother me. During spring, a variety of hornets and crickets would produce exceedingly loud sounds. Hundreds of crickets would stridulate in unison. Whether they were competing for a handful of females or celebrating something, I had no clue. Learning to transcend such noises took my meditation to another level altogether. Each time I crossed a hurdle, I gained better control over my mind, my senses.

Baboons also visited me. These fellows would freely jump onto the roof of my hut, hang on to the walls and peep through the holes. Sometimes, I felt they were intentionally teasing me, though that was not the case. It was just that earlier, this hut had never been occupied in the winter, so they were not expecting anyone inside. When they were clambering all over the hut, there was nothing I could do because I wasn't going to move and disrupt my meditation for some baboons.

When I was outside, I used to watch them swing from one tree to another. The sight always amazed me because

I never saw a baboon falling down. If I could have that mindfulness in my meditation, it would have been quite an achievement. In their case, it was in their genes. I suddenly realized that this is what I needed to do: shift the meditation from my conscious mind, where it was an effort, to the depths of my subconscious and unconscious states, where it was effortless. Over time, I would learn to do this.

Initially, when I started meditating, there were many wild animals around. I could hear boars snorting around at night but, as they smelled a human, they began shying away too. They never stopped coming though, you could easily make out from the trail in the snow the next morning.

The greater challenge, however, was not from the wild animals; it was from the rats, spiders, wasps and other insects inside my hut. Rats in the woods were as large as they were aggressive. Even though there were numerous holes in the walls and they were free to come in and go out through those holes, they kept on making new ones every day. As if imitating the expert predators, they would drag whatever they could get their teeth on into a corner and gnaw on it. No sooner would I sit down for my meditation than the rats would begin making noises. That constant sound of nibbling was a distraction at the beginning, but I learned to overcome it by persisting with my meditation. The rats often took the liberty of resting on my pillow while I meditated.

The spiders, unlike the rats, worked rather quietly. Every night, without fail, while I sat absorbed in my meditation, some persistent spider would weave a web from my head up till the roof. The roof of the hut was quite low. Once seated, there was less than 3 feet of a gap between the roof and my head. My mental state was such that, every morning, I would forget to check for the web. Whenever

I got up, I had to spend the next five minutes cleaning my face of the fine threads of the gossamer web they'd weaved from their spit.

As at Baba's ashram, I had the choice to destroy these creatures as well; it was not hard to do so. But these were not compassionate choices. I was here to practise compassion, and never so much as a mosquito did I ever hurt intentionally. Interestingly, not once was I bitten by a rat, stung by a bee, hornet or wasp, or attacked by any wild animal, and it wasn't a coincidence. Before the commencement of the sadhana, one of the rituals I had carried out involved praying to various divine energies for their protection. I invoked the gram devata, the protector of that region; the sthan devata, the protective energy of my immediate surroundings; and the vastu devata, the protective energy at the site of the sadhana. The lineage of the sages protects a true seeker, and this is, in fact, the primary purpose of initiation through a mantra. This was not all though. I had made a peace pact with all the living entities around me; they were all a part of nature just as I was, and made from the same elements I was. There was no room for disharmony.

Apart from the animals, there were other challenges to the body. A seeker goes through three types of obstacles: daihik, of the body; adhibhautik, physical; and adhidaivik, divine or environmental. My aches and pains were challenges of the body. The lack of food, resources and amenities were physical hurdles. The dangers posed by the wild animals or the unforgiving Himalayan weather were my environmental challenges; and there were plenty of all these.

High up in these mountains, massive storms arrived regularly: snowstorms, windstorms, rainstorms, hailstorms and blizzards. The sounds were deafening at times, as if unseen forces wanted to drive me out or the Divine was testing me, wanting to see if I still feared for my life. Or perhaps she was cheering me on, I couldn't be sure. Anyway, in these storms, you sense the magnitude of creation: one man, surrounded by gigantic mountains and dense forests, standing defenceless below thundering clouds and stormy, grey skies ... But what could nature possibly want from an insignificant being like me? Everything I was or had, including my body, was bestowed on me by the Divine. It was a liberating feeling to realize that I had nothing to lose, and therefore, nothing to be afraid of.

During the storms, the mighty winds would push and pull at the thatched roof of the hut, raising it by a few inches for a few seconds before violently slapping it back into place. Every time this happened, hoards of insects that had collected on the roof, both living and dead, would fall on me. The roof was harnessed by ropes; otherwise, it would have simply flown away. I had managed to slip a tarpaulin under the ropes, and placed heavy rocks on top to hold the tarpaulin in place. But the winds were too strong and, every time a storm came—almost daily for four months—they would displace the tarpaulin. If displaced, it was of little use. Pradeep would climb up on the roof and patiently readjust it after every storm.

On one occasion, there was a hailstorm. The sound of hail falling on the roof was deafening. I was glad that the wall behind me was properly covered with tarpaulin that had been secured with many nails. When I went out in the morning, I thought the wall looked somewhat different. It took me a few seconds to register that the tarpaulin was no longer on the wall but on the ground. In tatters. I figured that with the tarpaulin gone, rain would seep in through the wall. Since I sat by this wall, my bedding would also get wet.

This place had become unsuitable for me, but I was not prepared to leave under any circumstances. I looked up and said, 'Is that all you have? Show me what else you've got. I challenge you to move me from this place. I'll die but I won't move till I see your form. Why just the tarpaulin, take the roof, take the whole hut for all I care. You can torture my body, but my resolve is unshakable.' I wasn't feeling reverential but rebellious. This time, I decided to not have the tarpaulin replaced. I was prepared for whatever nature wanted to put me through. It rained umpteen times thereafter and water did seep in, but it never wet my bedding.

I remember the first time it snowed; there must have been about 12 inches on the ground. I started walking towards Pradeep's hut, but found myself unable to walk after about twenty steps. The chill in the snow was unbearable. I had driven in the snow, I had even played in the snow, but I had never walked in it with just my slippers on; I wasn't wearing socks. Walking another step became impossible; naturally, there was no place to sit. I stood midway between the two huts, completely stuck. I could not go back and I could not move forward. I was now in extreme pain and thought my feet would just fall off. Pradeep was under instruction that if I went into deep absorption, I would skip my meal and have it the next day instead. Therefore, if I collapsed now, Pradeep was unlikely to come looking for me, assuming I was in samadhi.

I wasn't worried about being attacked by wild animals if I fell down in the snow. And I wasn't afraid of dying. I just didn't want to leave my journey incomplete; I wanted to go right to the end. I looked up at the grey sky, the green trees around that were mostly covered in snow, the pristine peaks, and they were all quiet, indifferent. I looked up at the gods even though I wasn't expecting a miracle or help. I was carrying a walking stick with me, which I used because my knees still ached sometimes. I put all my weight on the stick and lifted my right foot to massage it with my free hand. But I could only do so for a few seconds because the other foot was giving up. This way, I alternated between both feet. I wanted to believe there was some relief but there was none. And now, my hands were completely numb and wet as well.

Chilly winds were blowing and the sky had become a dark grey. I thought that if I had to fall down anyway, I may as well move towards Pradeep's hut. If I called out for him, there was a chance he might hear me. It took me another twenty minutes but I made it to his hut alive. Once there, I could not feel my feet for a while. When the blood did start to flow again, my feet hurt so badly I wished I didn't have any feet. Not a nice thing to wish for.

After my meal, I had the challenge of going back to my hut. I told Pradeep that if it continued to snow like this, it would become impossible for me to visit him. In such an event, I would just munch on some dry provisions and try to survive. He packed some things for me to take back. I tied a polythene bag on each foot. Then, carrying the bag of provisions on my back, I began to walk back slowly. I was better prepared this time, and I made it. It was still hard, but nowhere near as hard as before. It's amazing what preparation can do. The right preparation is the key to the greatest attainments, the antidote to all fear, the seed of competence and confidence, I concluded.

It continued to snow but I managed to get to Pradeep's hut daily because I wore a pair of worn woollen socks the temple folks had given me; they offered me some respite from the snow. Even though they would get wet, it was still better to have a layer between bare feet and snow. At least I could walk. The snow decreased after January but patches of snow would remain outside my hut till April, and the surrounding peaks were covered till the last day I was there.

The winter made other aspects of daily life rather difficult as well, attending to the call of nature being the foremost. I had to go in the woods for the task, which was not a problem. But walking to the woods in the snow, and then squatting on the snowy ground as my feet became numb in a matter of moments, was not an adventure I cared for. In some ways, it was even harder than meditating. There, I could tame my mind through alertness and persistence. But here, my body was subject to the laws of nature.

Bathing in winter wasn't easy either. It was icy cold, of course, and it felt like I wasn't bathing but rubbing snow on my body. On the day it snowed for the first time, I had taken a bath at 1 a.m. When I sat down for my meditation, my body was like ice. I covered myself with a quilt and it took nearly two hours to feel the warmth again. Yet, there was something divine about bathing on clear nights in the Himalayas, especially when the moon was waxing. In the quietude of the wilderness, through the gaping holes of my hut, I could see the silvery mountains illuminated by the moon.

Sleep was another painful experience. Due to the extreme cold, not once did I manage to sleep with my legs stretched out. Further, if I accidentally made a swift movement and the quilt shifted ever so slightly, the biting wind that blew through the hut would make its way in, and it would take an hour to get back the warmth. As it was, I slept for no more than two hours at a stretch; if an hour was lost in feeling warm again, no time was left to rest.

My cotton quilt was rather small. Given the space, it wasn't possible to have a bigger one. I could either cover my feet properly or my head but not both, and I always chose to cover my feet. I discovered that I could not lie flat on my belly or back and have the quilt tucked under me on either side.

You might wonder why I didn't source more clothes or snow boots, or make myself more comfortable in the hut. Why did I choose to continue putting up with these obstacles? It was not because I wanted to punish myself or feel like a victim. The answer is rather simple. Our identification with the body is so strong that most people spend their lives simply taking care of the body. The body feels cold, let's clothe it; it feels hot, let's remove the layers; it's hungry, feed it; it's tired, give it rest. We become so preoccupied with fulfilling the body's many desires— cleaning, feeding, clothing, decorating and protecting it, that we become its slaves.

A true yogi must rise above the needs of the body. Just like an athlete must push herself to test her pain barrier, to test her limits, a spiritual aspirant must learn to control his body. When we start to tame the body and its needs, taming the mind becomes easier. The yogi must become indifferent to comforts until he has attained not only the state of emancipation but also learned to live in it.

Most of the difficulties I faced were linked to my body. Should I have been concerned about these hardships to the extent that I wanted to make myself comfortable instead of prioritizing my meditation? No, not in my world. 'If you want comforts, go sit in a serviced apartment,' I used to tell my body. 'If you want God, then shut up and meditate.'

I had always believed that my time in Baba's ashram was a preparation for my time here in the mountains. It was, to an extent. Living here though, I realized gradually that there was a lot more that the Universe wanted to teach me.

Confronting tougher physical challenges here was part of the process I was being put through: to test my resolve and courage, to hone my inner skills, to deepen my meditation. Finally, all my hardships were opportunities for surrender. Without total surrender to the Divine, I knew the Divine would never manifest before me.

Not everything was uncomfortable though. It was a real treat to be in Pradeep's hut because it was made of stone and kept nicely warm. Actually, both of us kept the fires going: he kept the outer fire alive while I kept the inner fire alive; both had a purpose.

Yet, there were ways in which Pradeep tested my patience. He was an incredibly talkative person, a complete contrast to me. The moment I would enter into his hut, he would start talking, and do so non-stop. He would tell me what the rats did last night, what provisions they ate up, what games they played, how they fought and so on. Imagine ending a long stretch of meditation and having to hear about rats right after.

But there was a lot more in Pradeep's repertoire. He would talk about his interactions with the villagers and what happened when he had gone down the previous day. Or he would tell me about his past, and the stories would criss-cross each other in a dizzying manner. I heard about his trip to a famous temple in Kerala where, while bathing, he realized that the water he was bathing with was the same water that was flowing back into the tap, so he was bathing with bathed water.

He told me how he had hurt his finger once, and it was badly crushed and bloodied. He asked his brother to take him to the hospital but his brother insisted that he wouldn't leave till he was dressed appropriately, and busied himself combing his hair, getting dressed, applying face cream and talc, etc. In desperation, Pradeep ran to the hospital by himself, and his brother arrived on his scooter after the dressing was done.

Thanks to Pradeep, I learnt about a certain cult in south India where four people would pin down a pig and a man would tear apart its stomach using nails. They would then dip bananas in the pig's blood and eat them. He told me the story of a certain barber in his village, who was watching cricket while cutting a child's hair. The batsman hit a six and the barber, in his excitement, accidentally snipped off the child's ear. 'What happened to the child?' I asked. 'He ran out, and his father came in and gave the barber a thrashing,' Pradeep said.

Once, Pradeep had a job in a charitable hospital where he had to boil 40 kg of milk every day. He would cool it down and eat all the cream from that milk. If Pradeep was tired of such tales, he went back to what the rats had done the night before. For instance, one day, he had accidentally touched the tuft of hair on his shaved head with buttery hands. That night, the rats thought fit to nibble on his hair.

When you have been meditating all night and you are both enraptured and exhausted from the intense experience, and you sit down to have your first and only meal of the day, these stories are not exactly entertaining. I needed silence and I begged for him to be silent, but the childlike Pradeep didn't understand. He simply could not remain quiet. You can't blame him though. I was meditating and working on stilling my mind; he was simply there to assist me. It is not natural for our species to remain in isolation or to be quiet for long periods, and it is the basic nature of the human mind to express itself.

Since I was living in solitude, perhaps only I could understand Pradeep's restless state of mind. He was outgoing and chatty, used to living in busy ashrams in bustling towns. Here, he was in terrifying solitude and had absolutely no one to talk to. In the woods, you can talk to the trees and to the wild animals and, if you can hold yourself together, you can talk to yourself. Those companions didn't fascinate him though, and admittedly, these weren't easy companions. So, he was compelled to talk to me.

There was no doubt that Pradeep's dedication for me was absolute. In fact, he had completely won me with his humility and devotion. But I felt frustrated with his meaningless rambles until it dawned on me that the Universe had planted him there to test and train me. The only way I could deal with this situation was by learning to remain calm and unaffected. How was this situation different from living in the world anyway? When I was there, life told me stories, good and bad. People had told me stories, long and short. The world had told me stories, true and untrue. My religion had told me stories, factual and fictional. Every experience life put me through was a story in some form. And now Pradeep was telling me stories.

I learnt that I didn't need to accept or react to Pradeep. I couldn't stop hearing but I didn't have to listen. Above all, the Divine lived in him as much as in me, so how could I reject him? Whatever life had to offer me through him was just fine. That's what love is: to be at ease. And that's what I learned with him around: to be at ease. I had never shouted at anyone, I had never had a fit of rage. But if there was any vestige of anger in me, I wanted to drop it completely. I had been given the perfect opportunity now. Extraordinary bliss with an anger-free mind is an epiphenomenon, one of the by-products of intense meditation.

༄༅།

Sitting cross-legged for long stretches of time wasn't hard for me, but doing so absolutely unmoving was a big challenge. In fact, it was one of the most difficult things I had ever done. I went through a phase of excruciating pain in my knees. Walking just a few steps was a daunting task as I couldn't even lift my feet due to the pain. I had two choices at that moment: to quit and go see a doctor, or persist. I chose to persevere and continued with my sadhana. I prayed to the sages, to the seers in the Himalayas, to my siddhas and asked them to help me. After about a month, the pain in the knees started to subside a bit. Still, I was sitting for ten hours at a time, and maintaining my concentration wasn't easy with the pain.

To reach the transcendental state, to go beyond the physical body, you have to reach a place where you can completely forget about your body. Bodily movements are highly detrimental to good meditation because they make you aware of your body. Therefore, it's absolutely essential to sit still in meditation because a still mind lives in a still body and a still body helps in stilling the mind; they complement each other. Just like you don't need the raft once you cross the river, these conditions no longer apply once an adept has mastered the art of staying in samadhi. At that time though, I was a seeker and not an adept. I hadn't yet learned to go into samadhi, much less stay in it.

Given all the challenges I'd ever faced, by far the most difficult one was the current one: to still my mind completely. Initially, every few minutes, my concentration would lose its sharpness. With persistence and alertness, however, those few minutes stretched to about half an hour, and then a little longer but, in any case, maintaining my concentration beyond the first hour proved rather difficult. My aim was to concentrate on Mother Divine without losing focus. If you don't know what I mean, simply think of an object. Try to visualize the image with your eyes closed. After a few seconds, the image in your mind will start to fade. Beginners can mentally hold the image for a few seconds; good meditators can do so for a few minutes; great meditators can do it for many minutes and the accomplished ones can do it for over four hours. I wanted to go beyond and meditate on Mother Divine all the time, twenty-four hours a day.

A loss of concentration is the biggest hurdle for a meditator, and the only way I knew to cross this obstacle was by not giving up. Persistence and patience had helped me achieve what I had wanted thus far, and I hoped these qualities would work again this time. They did, for my concentration began to stabilize gradually. I remember wanting to get up at times because the pain was unbearable or because I was extremely exhausted, but I would tell myself that this time would pass; even if I did anything else, time would continue to tick, so I might as well meditate.

Crucially, I knew I had to persist because the path of yoga was one of great discipline and rigour. Whenever I felt tired, I would remind myself that I did not leave my family, home and comforts to rest or relax; I left them to attain supreme bliss, to be one with God. I was often reminded of a devotional song my mother used to sing in Punjabi when I was a child: 'Bhagwan da milna sehaj nahin, puthi khal lahani paindi hai' (It isn't easy to attain God, one has to go through many hardships).

When you first start meditating, it is an act of the conscious mind and you have to make an effort to meditate. Once you start to master it, however, it takes on a new form. From an act, it becomes a state—a state of the subconscious mind. And, when you persist, it changes once again. No longer an act or a state, meditation becomes a phenomenon: it happens to *you*.

In the beginning, I struggled to keep my mind from wandering. Over time, it went to the other extreme. I had to make an effort to talk or think of something other than Mother Divine. Like an insect flying towards the light, my mind glided towards her constantly. I was not doing this as a conscious act anymore; it was happening to me. I was always dizzy and felt I was on a perpetual high. There are no words that can really define that euphoric state, but imagine listening to a lovely and soothing sound continuously. After a while, you become one with that sound.

∗∗∗

On 1 January 2011, I took a vow of truth. I decided that I would not tell a lie, no matter what. Till my last breath. It isn't easy to always speak the truth living in this world because truth can be painful, but it's a virtue and a discipline any sincere seeker must practise. Four days later, I was about to embark on a 150-day sadhana, and it would be the most important one of my life. This was the sadhana I had prepared myself for all these years. I was going to meditate on the quintessential mantra of Mother Divine, and I decided that the same mouth that uttered the divine name should not pollute itself by telling a lie. It was my commitment to God and to myself.

For the upcoming sadhana, I took out a piece of paper and drew a Sri Chakra yantra on it. As a Sri Vidya practitioner, I worshipped the Mother in the form of Goddess Maha Tripurasundari, one of the ten tantric Mahavidyas. This worship has three aspects: the yantra; the mantra of the Goddess; and sahasranama, her thousand names. Just as a child learning to swim may need floaters in the beginning, the tradition of Sri Vidya recommends using external aids like the Sri Yantra before turning completely inward, where the adept can then meditate solely on Goddess.

The word 'tri' means three and 'pura' means states. This goddess governs the three states of our consciousness. These three states are jagrat, wakeful; svapana, dreaming; and sushupta, resting or sleeping. These states find a resonance in multiple contexts. For instance, they refer to the three modes of material nature: sattva, the mode of goodness; rajas, the mode of passion; and tamas, the mode of ignorance. Further, 'tripura' relates to the three physical humours of the body: vata, wind; pitta, bile; and kapha, mucus. There are also three states of human existence: childhood, youth and old age. At the macro level, you have the three worlds: nether world, earth and heaven. At a micro level, it also pertains to the three states of mind: positive, negative and neutral. Ultimately, to go beyond all the states, the seeker must remain centred across all states, under all circumstances, firmly established in his or her devotion.

Sri Yantra is a geometrical representation of the energy field created by meditating on Mother Divine's form, and is a powerful aid in meditation. Within the Sri Yantra, more than 171 forms of energies are invoked before commencing the main meditation on the Goddess's mantra, which is chanted mentally. These energies elevate the seeker's state of mind and help it remain centred during and after the meditation so he or she can remain focused on the thoughts of Mother Divine.

Sahasranama, one thousand names, are used to call upon the Goddess in reverence and devotion. The idea behind chanting her thousand names is to cry out for her the way a child does for its mother; it is to become a child.

Young children are free from negative emotions like hatred, jealousy and malice—great obstacles for a devotee.

So, the Sri Yantra covers the visual and the energy aspect, the mantra is for the mental aspect and sahasranama is for devotion. When you are visually meditating on the Sri Yantra, when you are mentally meditating on the Goddess's mantra, when you are verbally chanting her names, you're practically living in her all the time. This is a state a seeker must reach to experience complete and unwavering oneness with God. I meditated on Mother Divine in this way for nearly twenty hours each day. Once you immerse yourself completely, there comes a time when you not only see the Divine but merge in the Divine, you attain complete union with God.

In my devotion, I had seen God as a being, a person almost, because it made it easier to surrender to a personalized form. Now, my yogic mind was beginning to see God as the essence of everything: the fragrance of the flower, the heat of fire, the chill in ice, the venom in a snake. The ultimate test of my devotion and my focus, though, was to see a manifestation of that essence. I wanted my concentrated thought to manifest before my eyes.

✦❀❀✦

My ability to sit unmoving for exceptionally long periods in meditation improved significantly with time. There came a stage when I stopped moving my head or my eyes to find out what the rats were doing on my lap or around me. From that stillness gushed forth the greatest fountain of bliss I had known. Perfecting the gaze is one of the subtle but promising signs of progress in meditation because when you are meditating deeply, even a slight movement of the eyeball is enough to bring your awareness back to the body, and it breaks the concentration.

My quiet and concentrated mind gave birth to an unusual phenomenon. I realized I could shut down my heartbeat at will. I didn't do any yoga, I wasn't aiming for it; it just happened naturally as a result of my extremely powerful meditations. I gained significant control over the involuntary functions of my body including the regulation of blood pressure, body temperature and pulse rate.

My consciousness travelled beyond my body and explored other planes of existence. However, I knew well that such experiences of astral travel could simply be a state of mind rather than any actual travel; the boundaries are blurred when you move through various states of consciousness. No doubt these attainments made me feel I was progressing, particularly because I was able to reproduce my experiences at different times of day. This gave me the confidence that there was cause-and-effect at work here, a scientific basis, rather than my imagination playing tricks on me. At the same time, I knew that these occurrences were distractions, and only the by-products of the meditation; they were not my goal.

As my sadhana continued, I was startled to discover powerful sensations building in my head. I did not take the idea of chakras very seriously and had stopped meditating on chakras years ago. Sensations emerged in those psychoneurotic plexuses on their own, and were strongest in my forehead and head.

I don't know of any word in any language that could possibly describe these sensations. How do you tell someone what a rose smells like? The only way to find out is to smell one. There was no pain or heaviness, only waves of deep bliss. I thought these sensations would go away but they didn't; in fact, I still experience them at all time.

I had never read about this sort of experience anywhere. One Buddhist text had mentioned these sensations briefly, but my yogic scriptures were quiet about it. What was happening to me? What did these sensations mean? I had no clue. But, despite all the powerful experiences I was having, I knew I could not get attached and had to press on with my sadhana. I still hadn't felt the Divine embrace, I was still desperate, I was still incomplete. I was still just me.

FOURTEEN

The Realization

Despite the intensity and concentration with which I meditated, and the desperation in my heart, I still hadn't seen a manifestation of the Divine. I didn't even know if the improvement in the meditation was any indication of my progress. I was already meditating to the maximum extent possible. I decided I had to be patient until the completion of my sadhana. On 13 February 2011, exactly forty days since I had started meditating on Mother Divine with the Sri Yantra and the mantra, something completely unexpected happened.

Just a few days earlier, I'd changed my routine and started meditating from 9 p.m. until 10 a.m. Around 5 a.m., while I was meditating with full awareness, a form appeared a few feet away from me. It was partially turned away from me.

In the past two decades, I had done tantric sadhanas of various devis, yoginis, yakshinis and apsaras, which were all lower energies of Mother Divine. At times, I had seen celestial forms, but these visions had been too short-lived to make any sense to me; at other times, I had encountered figures in dreams. This time, since I was awake, I thought I was seeing a celestial form like the previous occasions, and that it would disappear soon. Either way, I considered this a distraction that had appeared to disrupt my meditation.

With a firmer resolution and stronger equanimity, I brought my attention back to my meditation. The form didn't disappear; it continued to face the wall. Suddenly, it began moving its hands in a rhythmic way—now one hand moved and then the other, now the right arm swayed and then the left one swayed. Not wanting to get distracted by the hypnotic movements of the hands, I focused my attention on the mantra.

The form sat on the floor and faced me. I still didn't look at it properly. I was in deep absorption and determined to ignore this being. 'Aayo ji, aayo ji, Sarvanand Baba, aayo ji,' (Come here, come here, O Sarvananda, come here), a most mellifluous feminine voice called out to me.

Despite the fact that she had used the name Baba had given me, I took no heed and persisted with my meditation. A few moments later, she repeated the call. Thinking it was a nitya, female celestial being, one of the companion energies of Mother Divine, I continued to pay no attention. After calling my name for the third time, she turned towards me and looked at me directly. I couldn't disregard her any more. After all, she knew the name I rarely used or disclosed, and she was persistent. If this was an undesirable being or if she had come to just bless me, she would have disappeared by now; instead, this figure was sitting on the floor, cross-legged, just the way a mother sits with a child.

I did something I had never done before: I got up during my meditation. It was bitterly cold and I was wearing woollen socks. I quickly took off my socks so that I could greet the manifestation barefoot. There was not enough space to do a full-length prostration. Going past the Sri Yantra, I lay somewhat diagonally over the cold fire pit and offered my obeisance. 'I'm Sarvananda,' I said, and looked up.

Like wax that cannot withstand the heat, like darkness that disappears into light, I lost myself. What could I, a tiny drop, have known about the ocean? How could have I imagined that I would be looking into the effulgent eyes of the Creator, the Empress? Watching me was the one I had waited for my entire life. She had come.

I took in her fair face, the brilliance of her eyes, her small nose and full lips, the hair that flowed down to the ground like a black river. Her radiance was unbearable and I could not endure the sight of her. Just before I collapsed, she lifted me swiftly but gently and raised me above her head, as if I were a mere toy. I put my arms around her neck. When I glanced down at her, her flashing eyes annihilated every molecule of my existence as I had known it. I hid my face in her hair and entered a different world: it was an unending abyss as dark as her eyes were bright. Taking me through unimaginable spaces in the cosmos, she showed me the nature of duality, and how darkness and light, joy and sorrow, were inseparable. With a soft jerk of her arms, she made me tilt my head back, and now she was looking up at me. A myriad sentiments pushed me into an inexplicable state of consciousness. I hid my face in her hair again.

At my bidding, and because of my unrelenting and persistent cries, she had come; yet, now that she had, what did I have to offer her? Nothing. She, the owner of the Universe, sat on an uneven, dirty floor in a broken hut in the wilderness. Someone as magnificent as her should have been on her celestial throne. I didn't know how to welcome her, and wondered how a beggar was to offer hospitality to a queen. I had nothing pure enough to offer her. My heart, my body, my mind were all impure. I had no naivedyam, food offered with reverence. I did not even have flowers, but I wanted to give her *something*.

What could be purer than her own name, I thought. A eulogy to Mother Divine sprang out of me, gushing forth from the deepest recess of my heart. I raised my head, only just, and sang out as loud as I could. She gently swayed me back and forth one more time and gave me the most enigmatic smile full of compassion, love and mercy. She then put me down and disappeared. She was everything I ever wanted, all that I had ever known.

My watch read 5:08 a.m. I prayed loudly and cried heartily; I even laughed. For a while, I alternated between praying, crying and laughing. Gradually, I realized where I was and what had just occurred. To the non-believer or to the rest of the world, my experience may be dismissed as a hallucination or the product of a schizoid mind. And that's perfectly fine because, if someone had told me about such a thing earlier, I wouldn't have believed it either. There may be an imagination vivid enough to capture my experience but there are certainly no words apt enough to describe what I saw.

There was no doubt that what I had experienced was as real as the mountains, the hut, the floor I sat on, my very breath. The words, the touch, the play were all genuine, but I had no proof. Only someone who could enter my state of being could see my reality. In that one vision, I had seen the Primordial Principle, the Creative Energy.

❦

What I had come to seek, I had found. But I wasn't ready to leave just yet. I wanted to fulfil my vow of spending a certain period of time there and honour the Mother's mantra as well as the other divine energies who are worshipped as part of the tantric sadhana I was practising. Crucially, I needed to learn to live with the bliss that I had stepped into, or found within. I wanted to pray for the welfare of all sentient beings and pay homage to the lineage of siddhas I was a part of.

I began to experience an extraordinary bliss, and this was constant. But, at the same time, I was always dizzy. Sometimes, I felt as if someone was tugging at a point inside my brain; at other times, I got the feeling my forehead was being massaged. Daily functions such as walking, eating, talking to Pradeep and listening to his stories, became difficult. I had to learn how to absorb the powerful energies flowing through me. Thus, I decided to enter strict solitude for a hundred days. I needed this time to absorb the vision.

I informed Pradeep about my plan and his meticulous management made it possible. I changed my routine and began meditating from 7 p.m. until 4 a.m. If, once or twice a month, the villagers passed this way for hay, Pradeep would tell them to keep absolutely quiet. They maintained both distance and silence. During this period, I neither met nor saw anyone. Pradeep would wake up at 1 a.m., take a bath, say his prayers and prepare my meal before 4 a.m. He would come to the little temple near my hut, ring a bell and hide behind the temple wall so that we did not see each other.

I would then step out and go to his hut for my meal. Eating would take me nearly an hour because it was nothing short of a ritual for me. It was an opportunity to express my gratitude to Mother Nature, to the farmers who produced the grain and to Pradeep who cooked it. The digestive fire in the stomach is called vaishvanara. I would offer every bite to this fire, akin to the fire offering in a yajna. I still do, for that matter.

While I was gone, Pradeep would wait for me quietly or refill the water bucket in my hut. He'd also fix the tarpaulin on the roof in case a storm had blown it about at night. If I needed to communicate something, I wrote a note and left it in his hut.

Towards the end of March, I felt a shooting pain near my kidney. I was startled because I had already perfected my posture and wasn't expecting any more pains. I'd already been through excruciating knee pains, severe backaches, a tired body and aching arms and shoulders. What was this new pain? The middle plank of my bed had completely sunk, making it an uneven and unsuitable surface to sit on; perhaps my posture was the cause of the pain. I placed my pillow on the plank but this didn't help. I took an hour out of my sleep time and did some yoga asanas to stretch my body; this alleviated the pain just a little. It was becoming impossible for me to sit still for hours at a time, which is what I needed to do. I wasn't going to give up on my 150-day meditation though; I had to get rid of this pain.

Reflecting on the pain, it occurred to me that I hadn't seen the sun for nearly two-and- a-half months. I took my morning meals when it was still dark. I used to step out occasionally during the day, but I hadn't been out at all in the sunlight for nearly ten weeks now. I had been living in an extremely cold hut and didn't use a fire to warm myself. The next day, instead of yoga, I spread a mat and sat outside with my back towards the sun. That night the pain subsided to a large extent. I repeated the process for the next few days and the pain disappeared. I would never know what really caused it, but sitting in the sun relieved it.

Enjoying the sweetness of solitude, diving deep into the ocean of a still mind, I passed my days in deep meditation and crystal-clear awareness. I was acutely aware of everything around me: the sounds of hornets and wasps, a spider crawling on the wall, every drop of rain that fell. Any thought that emerged in my mind would not go unnoticed. This was truly an extraordinary level of awareness.

My intuitive faculties entered a new dimension. No matter what question I thought of, an inner voice gave me the answer. One day, during meditation, the same inner voice instructed me to visit Kamakhya temple. I would get sarvoch tantric diksha, the highest tantric initiation there, it said. I was reminded of Bhairavi Ma who had foretold this in Badrinath. I decided to visit Kamakhya after the completion of my sadhana. But, right now, I simply lived in the present moment. I was a boat sailing in an ocean of bliss; why, I was the ocean of bliss itself.

The silence within me was beyond description. Just as you churn milk and it turns into butter, and that butter can never become milk again, my mind had reached an irreversible state of peace and joy. I felt that to remain unaffected, no matter what the circumstances, to be unmoved by someone's birth, death, acceptance, rejection, praise or criticism—this sense of dispassion and detachment was arising from within me, without any effort.

I opened my notepad and scribbled in it: 'Self-realization is not an instantaneous act. We may have an aha moment but it is mindfulness that allows us to navigate the world with the utmost awareness of our verbal, mental and physical actions. It is one thing to grasp that we are not just the body, but it is another thing altogether not to react when someone hurts us. We may recognize that anger destroys our peace of mind, but to remain calm, no matter how strong the provocation—that is real realization.

Why did it take the Buddha six years to achieve liberation? If it was an instantaneous thing, he could have

had it in the first month. It took Mahavira ten years and
Ramakrishna Paramahamsa twelve years. The experiences,
lessons, insights add up, finally bringing one to the point of
realization. Water boils at 100 degrees Celsius but it takes a
little while to get to that temperature. The flame that heats
the water already holds the potential to burn as powerfully
as the sun, but it is the water that needs to come to a boil. The
soul or consciousness is ever pure; it is the conscious mind
that needs to reach boiling point, while the subconscious
has to imbibe the insights and the learning.

When Jesus was crucified, he didn't react. He simply
forgave. When Gandhi was shot, he didn't say, "Oh damn,
I've been shot! Who did it?" He said, "Hey Ram!" He
remembered his God. An epiphany or a sudden flash of
realization is assimilated and processed by the conscious
mind, but true liberation manifests deep in the subconscious
mind; it is this part of the being that has to be trained to
attain realization. Enlightenment teaches us how to live in
the world with grace, independence and joy.'

I wanted to write more but felt dizzy, and the words
swam before me. I did contemplate casting off my body
and merging in the Supreme Consciousness for there was
nothing more I wanted from the world. Life had given me
everything I could possibly seek, and more. I had become
what I had once sought; the seed of my individual existence
had perished in the soft earth of realization. My journey
was complete.

I had the choice of letting go my physical body but I felt
that dropping it would be selfish of me. I owed it to the
Universe to pass on what I had learned. I didn't want to
direct people but only guide them and walk with them, for
I firmly believe that we must learn to lead ourselves and
not be led by others. For that matter, even within, most of

us are controlled by our thoughts and emotions whereas it should be the other way around. Enlightenment turns the tables on us: we lead our thoughts and emotions.

It was time to redefine monkhood. Why should a monk be a burden to society? He should take responsibility for his own life and not depend on others for his needs. I wanted to be a monk, not a mendicant. I vowed never to accept donations for my personal needs. I did not want to build an organization with ashrams everywhere. I had to stay connected to my mission so I could enable other seekers to revel in the same nirvana that I did.

I was going to descend from the Himalayas on 3 June, and Pradeep informed the villagers that I would be coming to stay in the village for a couple of days. With my sadhana over, he had decided to go on a pilgrimage to the Jagannath temple. I would see him later in the year.

On 4 June, many villagers came to receive me. Babloo was very keen for me to stay at the Anasuya temple in Chamoli. I agreed, and also conducted a small ritual of kumari poojan, where girls below the age of sixteen are worshipped in the form of the Mother and offered gifts. After the ritual, everyone was given a meal. Forty people ate to their hearts' content food made from just two aubergines and one cauliflower; some people even got two servings. I'm not saying it was a miracle but I am expressing my surprise at the mysteries of Providence. Did the curry multiply? It doesn't matter; what does matter is that everyone went home well fed.

While leaving the woods, I felt pensive for a moment. I say pensive because this place hadn't just been quiet and lovely; it is where Mother Divine had come to me. It was a reflection of her. But, then again, what isn't her reflection? Besides, no matter how much I loved being there, I had to move on. Having eschewed the world, it was pointless becoming attached to the mountains. An attachment, it doesn't matter to what, is the cause of bondage and suffering anyway.

The trees and I had something in common: a sense of dispassion and detachment. They remained rooted to the ground and I remained rooted in my devotion. They didn't change their position, they didn't try and tempt me to return. I did not alter my stance either, for I realized that the only thing worth loving was the emotion of compassion and not the object of compassion. After all, parting from loved ones is inevitable. Both nature and I understood this. I thanked the woods and walked away with a joyous heart, once again immersed in the thought of Mother Divine.

FIFTEEN

Going Beyond

The powerful sensations in my head continued to affect me, and I still found it difficult to perform daily tasks. I wanted more time in solitude to be able to learn how to function in this altered state of being.

During my two-day stay at the Anasuya temple, I met a sadhu who asked me to come and visit him in his cave. I accepted even though I had no desire to do so. Babloo accompanied me the next day to his cave and clicked my picture with his phone. And so it was that I had a good look at myself after seven months. I had used a small mirror in the woods to put the tilak on my forehead, but it was too small to show my entire face. Unsurprisingly, I had grown a beard and my head needed to be shaved again. But, expecting sunken cheeks and pale skin, I was not prepared for how healthy I actually looked. I exuded an unfamiliar light, and my eyes had a strange glow. Was this really me?

On our way back to the temple, I found it difficult to walk because the sensations in my head were overpowering. I felt dizzy and looked down. All of a sudden, the ground disappeared from sight: my inner vision opened up to receive everything that there was before me—the ground beneath my feet, the leaves strewn about on the path, the trees, the person walking beside me, the black snake that just slithered past and dashed behind the rocks, the skies ... everything simply merged into me. Or did I merge into everything?

I could not walk a step further and sat down in the middle of the path. I told Babloo I was going into a deep trance. All this was happening was because I hadn't yet learned to absorb the state of deep tranquility I had reached and continue with my daily activities at the same time. Babloo asked me how long this state would last and I told him I didn't know. He was kind enough to wait there. After a little while, I felt more centred and we slowly walked back to the temple. The next day, I got tonsured and left for Haridwar.

After spending a few days there with Swami Vidyananda, I went to Kamakhya on 19 June. A big festival was due to start there after three days, and the crowd was building up. I had never cared for crowds. I made my way to the temple and rather than approaching anyone, decided to wait for five minutes in the temple compound. If the instruction I had received in the mountains was the truth and not just my hallucination, someone should approach me, I thought.

I had developed a method of conversation with Mother Divine back in the woods. I told her now that I was only going to wait 300 seconds by the clock. If no one came to me during this time, I would move on. I circumambulated the temple, came back to the compound, took the watch out from my pouch and began the five-minute countdown.

Less than two minutes later, a man clothed in a white kurta-pyjama waved at me. This action met all my conditions: I didn't initiate the interaction, it was within the five-minute limit and he seemed eager to talk to me. I walked up to him. Even though he was a Brahmin, he was sitting next to a tantrik clad in black, who turned out to be an aghori. Aghora is a school of vamachara tantra.

This aghori, however, like the majority out there, was more a boaster than a practitioner. Just as a good workman doesn't go around displaying his implements, a good aghori doesn't put his tools on display. This man, however, had made a circular firepit and laid out various items beside it: a human skull, bones, a box each of vermillion powder and turmeric, a metallic bowl and containers with grey as well as black ash, among other things. All this was merely to attract and fool people. After all, an aghori has no business conducting any rituals during the day; all aghora rituals are done at night, and a real practitioner is always discrete.

But the man's khappar, begging bowl, looked inviting. It was made from a kapaal, human skull. He let me inspect it, and I have to admit that it was highly energized. Just like bats can hear sounds over and above the range of frequencies audible to human ears, and they use this knowledge to move around, prey and protect themselves, a seeker practising sadhana develops a sensitivity to energy beyond what the average person can feel. An adept then uses this energy to help others.

When I held the skull in my hand, I experienced a flow of energy and could tell that this was not the skull of an ordinary man; it belonged to an aghori. I told him it was an amazing khappar. In response, he gave a proud smile and nodded. Then, in a flurry of words, he informed me that his 'god brother' had died of snake bite and, with their guru's permission, he had taken the head, skinned it, prepared it with the right rituals for forty days and served wine in it to his guru before making it his khappar.

Meanwhile, the Brahmin, who was the reason why I had even sat down beside the two men, wanted to know what was I doing at Kamakhya. Instead of answering his question,

I told *him* why he was there and what he had been doing the past few years. I went on to explain why his sadhana had not been successful. He could not hide his shock and began to weep. Without saying another word or acknowledging what I had just said, he got up and left.

I resumed my conversation with the aghori. Some fifteen minutes passed and I was beginning to feel that I was wasting my time. I was about to leave when the Brahmin returned. He asked me again, with much reverence this time, what had brought me here. Had I come for the festival? I simply said that I had come to do sadhana for a month and asked him if he could recommend an isolated location for me.

Suddenly, the Brahmin shouted out loud, 'Aye Sadhu!' and waved at another ascetic. This ascetic, also in white, came over and joined us. The two began chatting. A few minutes later, I told them I was leaving. Upon hearing this, the ascetic who had just arrived insisted that he wanted to offer me a meal. I wasn't keen but he wouldn't let me go. I agreed and the three of us went to his place, leaving the aghori behind since he couldn't leave his firepit unattended.

It turned out this sadhu wanted to do a mantra purashcharana, a rite of mantra worship and invocation that is done over a certain number of days. For example, to do a purashcharana of the Gayatri Mantra, a practitioner may decide to chant the mantra 1.2 lakh times over forty days. Therefore, the mantra will have to be chanted 3,000 times every day beginning at exactly the same time each day. There are four other components of a purashcharana: yajna, fire offerings; tarpana, libations of water or other alchemical concoctions; marjana, ablutions for self-purification done with the same concoction as the libation; and sadhaka bhojana, where Brahmins or other adepts are fed at the conclusion of the ritual.

Before this ritual can begin, other preliminary rituals need to be performed, including the invocation of the divine forces and protective energies. The seeker must be able to chant the preparatory mantras in Sanskrit. The condition of the preliminary rituals can only be waived if the purashcharana is done the tantric way or at the instruction of the guru.

This sadhu was doing a Vedic purashcharana and had to carry out the necessary rituals. He asked the Brahmin to initiate the process of worshipping the local deities, but the Brahmin didn't know how to conduct this ritual; he only practised tantra. The sadhu looked at me expectantly. I had renounced samsara, and a renunciant is not supposed to perform religious rites for others. Since he was a sadhu and a genuine one at that, I decided to perform the rituals for him.

Responding with gratitude, he served us delicious khichdi and asked me the reason for my visit to Kamakhya. I said I was looking for a suitable spot for a month-long tantric worship. He suggested a cave called the Siddhi Ganesh Gufa, which also contained a panch-mundi asana. Panch-mundi asana is a tantric seat made by burying the skulls of five different creatures, including that of a human, in the ground. The spot is then filled with ash from a funeral pyre along with turmeric and other ingredients. Sitting on the consecrated seat and invoking the Goddess through esoteric mantras is an important tantric practice.

When I heard about this cave, I immediately left his house and followed the directions he had given me. At a spot near a particular temple he had indicated, I had to descend a flight of 300 steps to reach the Siddhi Ganesh Gufa. It was by the banks of the Brahmaputra river.

Unfortunately, two sadhus were already living there. One of them was a tantrik absorbed in prayer. He was sitting not on top but in front of the panch-mundi asana, and had placed an oil lamp on the actual seat. As I stood waiting for the tantrik to finish his prayers, the other sadhu tried to engage me in small talk. I was least interested in this conversation and made to leave when the tantrik finished his puja and approached me. I told him that it was somewhat foolish to sit in front of the asana rather than upon it. It was like sitting next to a swimming pool and chanting water, water, water, hoping you would get wet. I suggested some minor changes he could make to benefit more from his sadhana.

He was deeply touched and asked me why I was there. Even to him, I just said I was looking for a quiet place to meditate. He suggested I meet a certain sadhu he knew who was a highly qualified tantrik. I was reluctant but he insisted, and offered to take me there.

The next day, we met the tantrik. In his mid-fifties, he was a vamachari tantric. When I sat in front of him, the same voice that had instructed me in the Himalayan woods to visit Kamakhya asked me now, in unmistakable terms, to share with him the purpose of my visit, including the tantric initiation I wanted to do. I did as I was told.

'I only know one adept qualified to give this initiation,' he said. 'He is really old and has not initiated anyone in the past twenty years. I cannot promise that he will initiate you, but you are someone I would definitely vouch for.'

I followed him through many small and narrow streets, which meandered this way and that until we arrived at our destination. I was ushered into a little house. The tantrik, lean and frail, sat on a mat facing the door, as if waiting for me. Near him sat a bhairavi who must have been in her eighties. She was strikingly beautiful and had an aura that was hard to ignore. Fair-complexioned with high cheekbones, she didn't have a single wrinkle on her face except for a few crow's feet, though her hair had turned grey. She knew very little Hindi and no English; her mother tongue was Assamese. She felt like a mother to me.

We offered our obeisances to the great tantrik. He looked at me and smiled. 'I'll initiate you,' he said, even before we had mentioned it. He knew exactly why we were there, but that didn't surprise me. After my vision in the mountains, nothing surprised me anymore.

As I was introduced to the bhairavi, who lived with the tantrik, she placed her hand on my head in blessing. The elderly ascetic enquired about my previous tantric initiations and sadhanas. He also wanted to know about my full name prior to renunciation, and about the guru who had given me sanyasa diksha. After I had responded to his questions, he said it wasn't possible to initiate me during the festival as Mother Divine, known as Kamakhya or Kamakshi here, was supposed to be menstruating at this time. Menstruation is a sign that the feminine energy is getting ready to procreate, that it is preparing for evolution. Linked directly to the lunar cycle, those five days are most auspicious for aspiring tantriks not only to transform themselves but to transmute their desires and emotions into transcendental energy — for their spiritual growth as well as for the benefit of humanity. The tantrik set the date of 29 June for my initiation.

I went to the cremation ground to ascertain the suitability of spending a month there. I also tried to find out about Bhairavi Ma. I shared her description with everyone I met, but no one had heard of her. Even those who were born and raised in Kamakhya, who had lived there for more than sixty years, did not know anything about her. Once again, I wasn't surprised.

The cremation ground was quite modernized. It had iron racks upon which they burnt the dead bodies. As soon as the body had finished burning, they would hose down the pyre to save wood. The place turned out to be unsuitable for my month-long sadhana: there were no traditional funeral pyres; it was too close to the main road; there was a busy Shiva temple nearby; and there were plenty of drugged and tipsy sadhus, pretending to be genuine tantriks, about the place.

Thanks to such sadhus, the world has misunderstood tantra and its essence. It is wrongly assumed that tantra is about tantric sex, tantric massage, tantric yoga and so on. This is not where tantra starts or ends. Tantra is an inner journey the practitioner undertakes to break the conditioning of the mind and move beyond the conditioned and egoistic self, so that he may see himself as he truly is. I was absorbed in these thoughts when one of the committee members of the Shiva temple approached me.

Upon finding out what I was looking for, he insisted I should stay at their temple for my sadhana. He even promised to make the necessary arrangements. I had a simple way of deciding the spot for my mantra sadhana: whenever I travelled somewhere, I sensed the place's energies. I always went with my first reading and it never failed me. I did not sense the right energy here and made up my mind to look elsewhere.

There was still time before my tantric initiation, so I decided to go to West Bengal, hoping to meet someone there who could talk to me about the sensations I was experiencing. I caught a train to New Jalpaiguri and then a shared taxi to Darjeeling. There, I visited three monasteries and had quite a revelation: the lamas were so occupied with daily chores, prayer rituals and the study of Buddhist texts that they had no time for meditation. Despite the fact that a faith is pure, and its teachings and philosophy profound and original, it will turn into a corpse if institutionalized. One is left with a brain-dead patient on life support; the only consolation is that the patient is still breathing. I felt sorry for the Buddha.

In one of the monasteries, I met a lama who told me about a senior lama doing rigorous meditation in the mountains. He spoke at length about this monk, who was now more than seventy years old. I was keen to meet him. I mentioned that I was well versed in mahamudra meditation, and had done countless hours of practise in it.

'Don't tell him this. He will get very angry with you,' he said.

'Angry?'

'Yes, because you practised it without any Buddhist lama initiating you.'

'Angry, did you say?'

'Oh yes, he will be really mad.'

At that moment, I decided I didn't want to meet their senior lama. If he hadn't overcome his anger all these years, what could he possibly share with me? What had he done in the past seventy years? What did he meditate on? What did he understand or let go? I quietly introspected on these questions. I was reminded of Naga Baba. Meditation, worship, praying, it's all useless if we are unable to go beyond what holds us back.

I went to Gangtok and visited a few more monasteries, but met no one who interested me. I went to the Rumtek monastery, far away from the traffic, noise and people, and met a lama who had spent his life teaching Buddha dharma. I spoke to him briefly about my journey and recent experiences. He put his hand on my pulse and I shut down the involuntary system of my body. He was greatly moved to feel no pulse. I thought I was about to find out something from him but he started prostrating before me instead.

The young monk who had introduced me to this teacher was present in the room. He was about to follow suit but I stopped them. He informed me that he had never met anyone who could do that, or sit in one posture for as long as I said I could. He also said that he did not know anyone who claimed to have deep physical sensations all the time.

This was a lama who knew Buddhist and Tibetan meditation like the back of his hand. He could perhaps give a far more enlightening and compelling discourse on meditation than I could, but here he was, with no experiential understanding. He knew the Tripitaka, the primary texts of the Buddhist canon, by heart. He could expound the Hinayana, Mahayana, Vajrayana vehicles of Buddhism. He was able to talk about sutras and the tantric path ... but how far can words take you? I shook my head, thanked him and left.

I was back in Kamakhya to meet the tantrik yogi on the appointed day. He was doing a kriya when I arrived, and there it was, lying in front of me: the severed head of a goat. It was the first time I had seen a severed goat's head from such close quarters, and it was a strange feeling. It almost seemed alive, its eyes half open and lips slightly parted, exposing some of its small teeth. I felt sorry for the poor animal. Had they tried to slaughter it in my presence, I would have certainly stopped them.

'Hold this between your thumb, index and little finger,' the tantrik said, and handed me a tiny vessel, no more than the size of half a thumb. He poured alcohol into it, made an occult mudra over it and asked me to drink the contents.

I'd never had alcohol. Also, I had fasted the day before as it was part of the initiation process, so I was a little concerned because I didn't want to lose my equilibrium. I expressed my reluctance and the tantrik said, 'It's not alcohol. It's an offering to Mother Divine that been consecrated. Even if you are to have a litre of this, you won't get drunk. And never call this alcohol, for it is one of the pancha-makara ingredients.'

Pancha-makara is a set of five ingredients used in tantric rituals, and each of them starts with the letter 'm'. The ingredients can be taken in their original form or substituted, depending on the nature of the sadhana. Along with the alcohol, I was given black oats, parched grain, coconut water and flowers. Finally, I took a sip of the alcohol—just enough to wet my mouth. I knew that this was the first and last time in my life I would have alcohol. In this way, I was initiated.

The bhairavi was wearing red that day. She looked beautiful, adorned with sparkling jewels and a red bindi on her smooth forehead. She had cooked a meal and wanted to feed me, but I was shy and didn't let her. The food was delicious and I savoured it, eating more than usual at her insistence. The couple blessed me before I left.

On an impulse, I went to Lava, a place in the eastern Himalayas, and meditated for a month in an isolated cottage. The sensations, however, did not subside. I was able to read and write now but not for long. One day, I entered into a deep meditation and prayed to Mother Divine for a solution. An inner voice guided me to do a yogic kriya of forty days. 'It will help you channelize your energies,' the voice said. 'You must harness the fire breath.' The breath of fire, also known as the breath from the solar channel, is the inhalation and exhalation from the right nostril. It significantly raises body heat and, therefore, is best done in a cold climate.

I went back to the northern Himalayas and meditated for the prescribed duration in a tiny hamlet called Rudranath, situated at an altitude of 14,000 feet. Rudranath is open only six months in a year because of the extreme weather conditions. I found a small hut in a desolate spot and decided to do my meditation there. Nearby was a beautiful Shiva temple. Though most temples have a Shivalingam, this one had an idol of Lord Shiva, a rarity.

I rigorously performed the yogic kriya. Exactly as the voice had predicted, the sadhana helped me harness my energies. The sensations did not decrease or die down though; instead, they intensified even more but were now concentrated in my forehead. My body no longer trembled and I found it much easier to read, write and walk. A stream of intense joy ran through my body like the Ganga flowing through the Himalayas.

When my kriya ended, I trekked down to a town called Gopeshwar and stayed overnight there. It was also time to let my loved ones know that they could see me again. I had promised them in my last email that I would re-establish contact soon after I attained self-realization. It was now time to honour that promise.

From my hotel room, I borrowed someone's phone and called my father.

'I'm sorry I left you like that.' These were the first words that tumbled out of my mouth. I had lost the right or the privilege to call him 'Dad'.

'That means you haven't understood me all these years, Swamiji. You went for a good cause and I have already accepted you as my guru. I offer a lamp and incense to your picture every day. You must treat me like any other disciple. You belong to the world now, Swamiji.'

While I wasn't surprised at his response because he had never interfered in my life, I was amazed by his reverence and acceptance. I wasn't expecting this. Actually, I wasn't expecting anything. I was simply keeping my promise to my family because I loved and cared for them. He handed the phone to my mother, and even though she was trying to sound strong and calm, her voice was choked. I also spoke to Rajan and Didi and told them I would visit them in a couple of weeks.

Finally, on 7 October, I visited the place I had once called home. It was here that I wanted to receive alms for the first time. All my close family members were present. In their eyes I saw the pain that my parting had caused them. When someone dies, you can find ways to console yourself, but when someone you love deeply disappears by choice and you don't know where he is, it is pain of an entirely different kind.

Invoking Shiva and Shakti in my parents, I sat them down on a high seat and paid obeisance to them. Every elderly man was my father, every elderly woman my mother. The whole world was my family but I had no home. I belonged to everyone now but no one was my own. I loved everyone unconditionally, cared about people and felt their pain equally. I was not the doer now but a silent observer. I felt like the quiet mountains—giant and still, and the vast sky—clear and endless.

When I spoke to my father a little later, his first question was: 'What message do you have for us?'

'The universe is trillions of years old, our galaxy and planet are billions of years old. The human race is a few million years old, while the average human life is seventy years. It's a very short life. It must be celebrated, it must be lived. Life is not a challenge that needs to be faced. Nor is it an enemy that needs to be fought. For that matter, it's not a problem that needs solving either. It's a flowing river, and all we need to do is to flow with it,' I said. 'Live. Love. Laugh. Give.'

I also met my mother privately. Like my father, she bowed before me from a distance. I folded my hands and asked her to never do that again because no matter what had I become or attained, she would always be my mother. No doubt, I had found the lap of Jagajanani, Mother Divine, but the lap of my janani, mother, was no less transcendental. I peered into her slightly swollen and red eyes. Behind her tender smile, I could see the tears she had just shed on seeing me in my monk's robes. She was trying to speak but her words didn't seem to come easily.

'The prediction has come true, word for word,' she said softly.

'What prediction, Ma?'

She told me her conversation with the mystic before I was born.

'Why didn't you tell me this earlier?' I said.

'I never wanted to be a hurdle on your path. But, somewhere within, I had this hope that if I didn't talk about it, perhaps it wouldn't happen.'

'Are you sad that I renounced?'

'How can I be sad if it makes you happy, Swamiji? Today, I can say to the world that I'm the mother of a saint.'

Epilogue

Enlightenment does not mean you have to live like a
pauper. It does not mean you have to subject yourself
to a life of hardship and abstinence. On the contrary, to be
enlightened means to live in the light of love, compassion
and truthfulness. It means learning to live without
reservations and inhibitions. I have seen many teachers
and sadhus who teach renunciation and detachment,
yet are deeply attached to their own ideas, agendas and
possessions. I have met young monks from monasteries
who visit restaurants and shops, eager to enjoy things they
can't afford. Rather than begging or being a poor monk
eyeing material comforts, it is far better to live in the world
and be detached.

Your knowledge of rituals and the scriptures, the time
you spend in places of worship, the money you raise for
religious causes—such things, I am sorry to tell you,
have absolutely no connection with God unless the heart
is open to the Divine. Such acts will not even lead to an
independent way of thinking, let alone enlightenment,
unless you understand well that the objective of religious
acts is to purify yourself and cultivate compassion and
gratitude. The more you get attached to a cause, religious

or otherwise, the more you restrict your own freedom. The most inflexible people I have met are generally the most 'religious'. Religion is our creation. It is the middleman who over-promises and under-delivers and, what's more, it rarely connects us to the right supplier.

Some scriptures say that this world is an illusion, or that after death there is a heaven and a hell. There may be an underlying substantive reality—the invisible essence in everything visible—but that does not make this world an illusion or unreal. The pleasure you experience during moments of intimacy, the joy you feel when your child smiles, the pleasure you get when you taste success, the high you experience when you attain your goal ... these may be temporary but they are not illusory. The satisfaction and nourishment we get from eating food is a temporary experience too, but we do not stop eating or decide to go in search of a miracle pill so we never have to eat again.

The world may be temporary but that does not make it unreal. Nothing is absolute or permanent, anyway. The reality is that everything in creation is in a state of constant transformation; everything is interconnected and interdependent. Wisdom speaks only to those who are open to the truth, and insight does not speak at all; it just dawns. So, I cannot give you any insight, it must come from within. I can only share my own learning.

Krishna, Christ, Buddha and Muhammad shared their knowledge and their truth with the world, but they did not invent the light bulb, create fire, or invent tools for agriculture. We owe our gratitude to the minds who gave us these gifts as much as we do to those who have imparted great spiritual truths to us. Are we to say one is better than the other? We need both spirituality and science. We depend on religion and theology because we have lost faith in ourselves and in our fellow humans. As a result, we need external pillars to support ourselves. Self-realization is removing yourself from that support structure. You no longer require the pillars; in fact, you become a pillar of divine love and light.

This is a precious life and all religions, for better or worse, are mere concepts. The sooner you wake up to this reality, the quicker you rise above them. But truth is not a one-size-fits-all. It's a personal matter, a private affair. Einstein found it in a laboratory. Buddha found it under a tree. Edison found it in a light bulb. Socrates exemplified it by drinking hemlock and Christ exemplified it on the Cross. Bill Gates found it in Microsoft and Steve Jobs found his in Apple. What is your truth?

The eternal truth is that you have the right to live your life to the fullest. Every moment. This is the least you deserve. The fact that you are breathing and living means nature wants you, life wants you. As long as you have a compassionate view and you are not hurting others, everything—well, almost everything—is okay. Listen to your inner voice. This voice is the purest voice you will ever know. Your truth is also the greatest religion, the highest God. A sense of fulfilment comes from walking your own path. For some it may be meditation, for others it may be music, dancing, painting, writing or reading. Find what makes you happy and pursue it.

I am not your traditional sadhu or a celibate monk. I am not a ritualistic priest or a rigid preacher either. I just am my own truth, bared before you, without any expectations or agenda, free for you to interpret as you like. I invite you to seek your own liberation by finding what matters to you and by living your life to the fullest. Rewrite your rules, redefine yourself. Don't let life slip you by. You are a master of infinite possibilities.

I've given you my truth. Go, discover yours.

Acknowledgements

I t is beyond the periphery of my expression to acknowledge the contribution innumerable people have made in my life. Just like the body is a colony of countless cells, my life is simply a congregation of the good done by others. This memoir, and my every breath, is an acknowledgment of their beautiful and bright strokes on the canvas of my heart.

My deepest gratitude to Mother Earth for patiently bearing me and providing for me. I'm indebted to every single living entity, for we all are interconnected and whatever we do has an impact on everyone else. The bounty of love and peace bestowed on me by the Universe is, therefore, a direct result of the noble acts of the people around me.

There are those who taught me what I needed to learn, who forgave me for my mistakes, who loved me immensely and who supported me unconditionally; I'm grateful to you.

It is not possible for some words on a page to recognize the contribution of everyone in my memoir. Nevertheless, I must highlight those who have worked incessantly to make this book a reality for a bigger cause.

Writing is not my forte. I realized this after I was done writing the first draft of my memoir, which, to be honest with you, read more like the operating manual of a microwave oven than a book because I had simply documented the events of my life. What's even more noteworthy, I thought I had done a good job. But then it went into the hands of Ismita Tandon, an adorable person and my first editor, who helped me transform the manuscript. Thank you, Ismita, for your unwavering confidence in Swami and his work.

I was considering self-publishing my memoir when Ismita sent the manuscript to Rukmini Chawla Kumar, a commissioning editor at HarperCollins India, who expressed her interest in publishing it. I thought the editing was near done, but then Rukmini edited the manuscript with an uncanny attention to detail and worked her magic. If there's a literary equivalent of pulling a rabbit out of a hat, she did exactly that. Thank you, Rukmini, for doing the wonder only you could do.

Anju Modgil in Canada deserves a special mention for diligently going through each and every word of my early draft and raising flags wherever more clarity was needed. Thank you, Anju, for your relentless enthusiasm and unparalleled devotion.

I would like to thank PB, Oswald Pereira, Navjot Gautam, Harpreet Gill, Suvi Gargas, Meenakshi Alimchandani, Kaley Belakovich, Shweta Gautam, Manik Gautam and Kanishka Gupta for their comments. And my gratitude to the two swamis, Swami Parmananda and Swami Vidyananda, who listened to parts of my memoir and gave important feedback. My heartfelt thanks to Ganesh Om for his profound and insightful remarks.

My thanks to the awesome cover designer, Alexander von Ness, and to the celebrated artist, Min Wae Aung, for granting us the permission to use his painting for the cover. Thanks also to Bonita Shimray at HarperCollins for further creative input in the cover design. My gratitude to Rajan Sharma for funding and managing the artwork.

I would like to thank Sridevi Rao as well as the sales and marketing team at HarperCollins, notably Sameer Mahale, Iti Khurana and Hina Mobar, for their priceless inputs.

This is not all though. To ensure this book reaches more readers, a few other people offered much assistance. In particular, my gratitude to Sanjeev Madan, TR Ramachandran, Sarala Panchapakesan, Neeta Singhal, Prasad Parasuraman and the Unnati Foundation, Bangalore.

Finally, none of this would have been possible without Vivek Dhume, who provided generous and unconditional financial support for the whole endeavour, and Narender Anand, who executed it flawlessly. Thank you, both. Swami's indebted.

Now you know what I mean when I say that this book, and my life, are a result of the good done by others.

Made in the USA
San Bernardino, CA
16 March 2020

65689370R00163